More praise for
Kitty Genovese

"Researched with considerable care . . . first-rate." —*Washington Post*

"Industriously comprehensive." —*Wall Street Journal*

"Cook manages to maintain an impressive level of tension. . . . [M]oving . . . compelling." —*Christian Science Monitor*

"Smart . . . suspenseful. [Cook's] reporting . . . is rich and deep." —*Tampa Bay Times*

"Cook's restoration helps make Kitty human, not merely iconographic." —*Cleveland Plain Dealer*

"Cook debunks the whole parable of the 38 Bad Samaritans and puts forth the real story of what happened." —*AARP Bulletin*

"Intelligent, superbly researched and truly unsettling . . . one of the best true crime books I've read in the past few years." —*Sunday Herald* (UK)

"Well-written and . . . gripping." —*Times* (London)

"This is not a good book. This is a GREAT book. I don't think I've read its compelling equal in twenty years. Every page reveals astonishing new facts about one of the most paralyzing events in the flawed soul of the American character. This is modern history at its storytelling best, ignored at the reader's peril." —Harlan Ellison

"Finally, Kevin Cook's book connects all the dots, giving us answers instead of myths and half-truths. This is a must-read."

—Curtis Sliwa, founder of the Guardian Angels

"Kevin Cook rips the cover off an enduring urban myth. He's done a first-rate reporting job, one that delivers the truth at last about an infamous murder that came to define an age."

—Kevin Baker, author of *The Big Crowd* and *Paradise Alley*

"For too long the savage 1964 murder of Kitty Genovese in New York has been viewed as an urban horror story that has morphed the victim into a pop culture icon. At last that myth has been debunked and the truth behind this sensational crime revealed. In this well-researched and skillfully written book, Kevin Cook convincingly recasts the story and reveals what really did take place that night a half-century ago in Queens as well as events before and after the brutal act was committed. In so doing, Cook brings Kitty Genovese to life in the context of her times in the turbulent 1960s."

—Michael Wallis

"*Kitty Genovese* is a book you can't help but devour."

—Terri Schlichenmeyer, *Newton Citizen*

"A seamless account using a balance of drama, detail, analysis, and just enough graphic description to satisfy . . . curiosity."

—Susan K. Perry, *Psychology Today*

"Cook cracks the case with a no-holds-barred, reality-TV look at a local crime that went viral 1960s-style and the media hype and public furor swirling around it."

—Tammy Scileppi, *Times Ledger*

 W. W. NORTON & COMPANY
New York London

KEVIN COOK

Kitty Genovese

The Murder, the Bystanders,
the Crime That Changed America

For information about permission to reproduce selections from this book,
write to Permissions, W. W. Norton & Company, Inc.,
500 Fifth Avenue, New York, NY 10110

For information about special discounts for bulk purchases, please contact
W. W. Norton Special Sales at specialsales@wwnorton.com or 800-233-4830

Manufacturing by Courier Westford
Book design by Ellen Cipriano
Production manager: Devon Zahn

Library of Congress Cataloging-in-Publication Data

Cook, Kevin, 1956–
    Kitty Genovese : the murder, the bystanders, the crime that changed America /
Kevin Cook. — First edition.
        pages cm
    Includes bibliographical references and index.
    ISBN 978-0-393-23928-7 (hardcover)
    1. Genovese, Catherine, –1964. 2. Murder victims—New York (State)—New
York—Biography. 3. Murder—New York (State)—New York—Biography.
4. Witnesses—New York (State)—New York. 5. Police—New York (State)—New York.
I. Title.
    HV6534.N5C67 2014
    364.152'3092—dc23
                                    2013041176

ISBN 978-0-393- 35057-9 pbk.

W. W. Norton & Company, Inc., 500 Fifth Avenue, New York, N.Y. 10110
        www.wwnorton.com

W. W. Norton & Company Ltd., Castle House, 75/76 Wells Street, London W1T 3QT

1 2 3 4 5 6 7 8 9 0

To the memory of Catherine Genovese,
who might have celebrated her seventy-ninth birthday in 2014

Contents

Master, what shall I do to inherit eternal life?

He said unto him, What is written in the law?

And he answering said, Thou shalt love the Lord thy God with
all thy heart, and with all thy soul, and with all thy strength,
and with all thy mind; and thy neighbor as thyself.

And he said unto him, Thou hast answered right: this do, and
thou shalt live.

But he, willing to justify himself, said unto Jesus, And who is my
neighbor?

—Luke 10: 25–29

Kitty
Genovese

Prologue

You heard her cry out. Not the words, maybe, though the words were loud. "Oh God he stabbed me. Help me!" But you'd been asleep. Your windows were shut against the cold. It's three in the morning, for God's sake. The sheer shrill sound, though—you couldn't miss that. Her shouts were loud enough to wake people on both sides of the street. So maybe you get up too. Maybe you pad to the window in the dark to see why somebody on Austin Street is screaming bloody murder.

Do you call the police? About a girl shouting? They'd laugh. Twenty to one it's nothing—a lovers' spat. A wife or girlfriend getting smacked, which is a lousy thing but not exactly news, not on Kew Gardens' worst block a couple of hours after last call at Bailey's Pub.

Except that this isn't regular pissed-off drunk hollering. This is panic.

"Help me!"

On the sidewalk outside the Austin Book Shop, a man bent over a girl. See him? She's on her knees, doing . . . what? Trying to get up. It's hard to tell, looking through a smudged window and the bare branches of the pin oaks and sycamores lining the street.

Somebody yells, "Leave that girl alone!" More lights pop on up and down the block. The girl and her attacker, if that's what he is, are alone on the sidewalk under a streetlamp, visible to dozens of bleary-eyed people in the nine-floor Mowbray Apartments on one side of Austin Street and the two-story faux-Tudor apartment building on the other. Somebody must have called the cops by now. And look, the guy's leaving, slipping into the dark. Leaving the girl behind. She gets up. Not screaming anymore. She gets up and walks past the shuttered TV-radio store with its starburst sign in the window: HIT RECORDS! *45 RPM 39¢*. Stepping slowly, but not like a drunk. More like sleepwalking. One wobbly step after another, like she's in a dream. She walks to the corner of the Tudor building, goes under the drugstore sign and then around the corner, out of sight.

It's quiet. A minute goes by. Windows going dark on both sides of the street. There's no sign anything happened, just a few dark spots on the sidewalk that might have been there before. Five more minutes pass. All over, nothing more to see.

Until he comes back. The same man? With a hat on now, a fedora with a feather in the brim. He strolls past the railroad station to the Tudor building, looking in doorways like he left something behind. Trailing the girl around the corner, carrying something in his hand. Looking for her? It's so hard to see.

Your phone's right there. . . .

1

More Than a Name

This is the story of a crime that lasted forever. It must have seemed endless to the victim, attacked in the middle of the night by a figure springing from the dark, the primal human nightmare. By the wall clock in the Long Island Rail Road station next door, the crime lasted about thirty-three minutes. One thousand nine hundred and eighty seconds—nearly as many heartbeats, fewer breaths. By another reckoning, however, a crime that began half a century ago hasn't ended yet. There was a trial, a verdict, and a sentence, but in a larger sense the case is still being argued, interpreted, reinterpreted, misinterpreted. The perp went to prison, but what about the neighbors who ignored the victim's cries for help? What were they guilty of? In the most popular account there were thirty-eight of them. In another there were thirty-seven. In another there were only two or three. In yet another account, modern life itself is to blame for what happened between 3:19 and 3:52 a.m. on Friday the thirteenth of March 1964.

Timing was crucial to the story from the start. The crime went practically unnoticed at first. Then, two weeks later, it was front-page news. Why?

After going viral, 1960s-style, through newspapers, magazines, television and radio editorials, Sunday sermons, dinner-party conversations, schoolyard rumors, and back-fence gossip, the Kitty Genovese story prompted months of local and then national soul-searching. Over the years the story became a fixture in thousands of high school and college psychology classes despite the fact that the version of it taught in those classes, the version almost everyone accepts, isn't true. Maybe that view of the crime endures *because* it isn't true, because it boils a complex, troubling story down to a single simple question: How could all those people watch what happened to her, and do nothing?

And a corollary: I would have helped her . . . wouldn't I?

This book is not a retelling of the usual version of what happened to Kitty Genovese in 1964. It is an attempt to tell the whole truth. I want to tell you a story that has not been told before. I want to tell you why the events of that cold night in Kew Gardens, Queens, have been misunderstood for a half a century. Just as important, I want to show that Kitty Genovese was more than a name in a newspaper. She was a strong-willed, generous, adventurous, troubled but optimistic, hard-working, fast-driving, living, breathing person who was not abandoned by her neighbors on the last night of her life. At least not by all of them. I want to tell you where Kitty came from, what she liked doing, what she hoped to do with her life, how she talked, worked, loved, and played, and how she came to be alone on the sidewalk across from the Kew Gardens railroad station fifty years ago.

...

Start with a little girl in a first communion dress. It's the spring of 1943, the heart of the war years. Brooklyn's smoggy sidewalks are crowded with cars and trolleys, with matrons, grandmas, boys, girls, and young women, but few young men. Many of the young men are fighting Hitler in Europe or Tojo in the South Pacific. Mothers and fathers sit up at night listening to war reports and President Roosevelt's fireside chats, praying they never get the Western Union telegram every soldier's parent dreads. In the Borough of Churches, full of the music, cooking smells, jokes, accents, and sharp elbows of second- and third-generation immigrants, women still dress for church in skirts and gloves that match their hats. Their husbands put on jackets and ties when they go to the city, meaning Manhattan. Some summer weekends they take the kids to Coney Island.

With a population of three million that nearly matched Chicago's, Brooklyn was crosshatched with ethnic neighborhoods, more a griddle than a melting pot. Brooklyn Heights was mostly white and Protestant. Bedford-Stuyvesant was home to a growing number of Negroes, which worried some of the Irish, Italian, and Jewish residents of other neighborhoods. Smaller Greek, Polish, and Scandinavian enclaves filled the cracks between communities. In working-class Park Slope, Italian and Irish families gathered to pray at the Church of St. Augustine, a brown-sandstone castle on Brooklyn's Sixth Avenue. Huge, cruciform St. Augustine's, built from 1888 to 1892, stood so tall that its bell tower's midmorning shadow fell on tarpaper roofs two blocks away. Walt Whitman's *Brooklyn Daily Eagle* called the church "one of the finest examples of Gothic architecture in the country." Morning light flooding through its vast stained-glass windows made martyrs' faces glow and cast shadows in rainbow colors on the church's terrazzo floor. A two-story pipe organ with 1,674 pipes droned hymns that rose past granite columns toward the nave's vaulted ceiling. A child couldn't help feeling small under that hundred-foot ceiling.

One Sunday each spring, a Mass at St. Augustine's was set aside for the parish's second-graders to receive their First Holy Communion. The children rehearsed for weeks, kneeling and making the sign of the cross, sticking out their tongues ("Respectful—no crossed eyes," the nuns said) for unconsecrated hosts so onion-skin thin they melted on the tongue like sugar ("No chewing," the nuns said; it was wrong to chew the body of Christ). The children were told not to expect Sunday's consecrated wafer to taste any different from the "practice host" of their rehearsals even though it would truly be the flesh of our Lord, an idea that jostled uneasily in some of the children's minds with thoughts of stickball, jacks and marbles, hopscotch, double-dutch jump rope, war movies at the Prospect Theatre, and the gumballs and lemon drops under glass counters at Morris's Candy Shop.

On the day of her first communion, Kitty stands perfectly still while her mother pins a lace veil to her hair. Kitty steps from her family's brownstone flat to a sidewalk dotted with blots of old chewing gum. Pigeons scatter. In her white-on-white communion dress she could pass for a miniature bride. She is seven years old.

Catherine Susan Genovese was the first child of Vincent Andronelle Genovese, who ran Bay Ridge Coat & Apron Supply Company, specializing in aprons for the restaurant trade, and his wife, Rachel, née Giordano, a homemaker. Some of their relatives pronounced the family name the old-country way, *Geno-vay-say*, but Vincent and his family, while proud of their heritage, were also proud to be as American as pizza pie. They answered to *Geno-veez*. They lived in a four-floor, four-family row house on St. John's Place, a block and a half from St. Augustine's. Brooklyn's Prospect Park in those days was nothing like today's trendy Prospect Park with its wine bars and three-million-dollar brownstones. Even today the Genoveses' old neighborhood is a lower-rent part of Park Slope, dotted with liquor stores, laundromats, nail salons, and abandoned grocery carts liberated from Key Foods supermarket. The flat-faced row house where Vincent and Rachel Genovese raised five children was less imposing than the brownstones across the street with their cut glass–windowed doors atop curved stairs. Number 29 St. John's Place had no stoop, just a porch behind a wrought-iron railing. The block was mostly Irish and Italian, but the Murphys and O'Connors lived up the street; the Genoveses shared the row house at 29 St. John's with the Maiella, Mastrorocco, and Ruvolo families. Inside, a dimly lit vestibule led to a narrow, carpeted stairway. There was a skylight in the roof, but only a sliver of sun found its way to the ground floor. The four large apartments were stuffy in the summer, steamy with the hiss and clatter of radiators all winter, alive with voices, busy lives, high hopes.

Catherine, called Kitty, was the eldest of five Genovese kids: Kitty, little Vincent, Susan, William, and Francis. Kitty was the talker, bright-eyed and full of pep. Popular in school if no great shakes as a student, she got As and Bs in the English and music classes she liked, and by eighth grade the boys were noticing her looks. Kitty Genovese might not have been a teen beauty to rival Elizabeth Taylor or even Edythe Marrenner, who had preceded Kitty through the local public schools before moving to Hollywood and changing her name to Susan Hayward. Kitty's hair was shapelessly cut and her eyebrows, before she began plucking them, were heavy enough to draw comments from mean kids. Still she made a lasting impression on people she met. "Kitty was attractive, but there was more to her than looks," says Angelo Lanzone, an old friend. "Kitty had charm."

From 1949 to 1953 she attended the all-girl Prospect Heights High School, a sandstone rectangle that covered a city block. Today it houses four high schools. Across Washington Avenue lay the Brooklyn Botanic Gardens and Prospect Park. From the south, when the wind was right in April, May, and June, she and her classmates could hear cheers coming from Ebbets Field in Flatbush, six blocks away, as Gil Hodges, Jackie Robinson, Duke Snider, and the Brooklyn Dodgers delighted fans all summer before breaking their hearts in the fall. After winning the National League pennant in 1949, '52, and '53, the Dodgers lost the World Series to the Yankees each time. In '51 the Giants' Bobby Thomson shocked them with his "Shot Heard 'Round the World." The borough was known for its slapdash Brooklynese peppered with the *dese*s, *dem*s, and *doze*s of loud Dodgers fans who fell temporarily silent each time Dem Bums lost again. In the words of one newspaper poet, a Yankee fan for sure, "The lonely men in Brooklyn bars / They hear the wind between the stars." Yet hope sprang eternal in Flatbush, where every October the Dodgers' fans cried, "Wait till next year."

At seventeen, Kitty stood five foot one in her patent-leather shoes. Dressed in a pleated skirt and neatly pressed white blouse, she waded into a tide of similarly dressed girls in the crowded halls of Prospect Heights High. School photos show a teenager with a short, puffy haircut, heavy eyebrows, and a solemn expression—except for a picture in which she beams like she just played a joke on you. In her graduating class of 712, twenty-three Prospect Heights seniors were named Class Celebrities of 1953, including *Kitty Genovese—Class Cut-Up.*

Nineteen fifty-three was what the newspapers called a "year of change." In January, Dwight Eisenhower succeeded Harry Truman as president. Joseph Stalin died in March, ending the second chapter of Soviet history. In June, following the death of England's King George VI, his daughter, twenty-seven years old, was crowned Queen Elizabeth II at Westminster Abbey in the first televised coronation.

Two weeks later, the Reverend Martin Luther King Jr., twenty-four, married Coretta Scott, twenty-six, on the lawn of her mother's house in Marion, Alabama. The next day, Julius and Ethel Rosenberg were executed in Old Sparky, the electric chair at Sing Sing Prison in Ossining, New York. Julius died instantly, but his wife survived three applications of two thousand volts, almost twenty times the charge delivered by a household electrical socket. Smoke rose from Ethel's head and from the leather cuffs that bound her wrists to the chair. Still her heart beat. The executioner zapped Ethel twice more before his job was done.

Six days later, on June 25, 1953, Kitty Genovese graduated from high school.

She was two weeks shy of her eighteenth birthday. She must have shown some interest in crime and punishment because her 1953 high school yearbook, *The Cardinal*, carried a fanciful class prophecy featuring this prediction: *We take you to the steps of City Hall where Police Inspector EVELYN FANTI is about to present citations to patrolmen KITTY GENOVESE and PHYLLIS TROMBOLI for their many faithful years of service and for helping our fair city crack down on crime.*

Brooklyn was changing as its ethnic neighborhoods expanded and collided. Postwar prosperity brought social mobility to men like Vinny Genovese while others lost their jobs as local factories closed or moved away. Black families were moving from Bedford-Stuyvesant to traditionally white areas where renters of various ethnicities shared little but a deep distrust of any Negro who wasn't Jackie Robinson or Roy Campanella. More than 135,000 Brooklynites fled to the suburbs of Long Island and Westchester County between 1950 and 1957, the year the Dodgers abandoned Brooklyn for Los Angeles. The 1950s also brought an uptick in crime. Kitty had barely started dating boys, a rite of passage that filled her with troubling longings and queasiness, when her mother witnessed a murder on the street. Rachel Genovese practically walked into a shooting; she was close enough to see the victim's blood filling cracks in the sidewalk. That was enough urban crime for the Genoveses. Vinny had worked hard and saved until he could buy his family a ranch house in New Canaan, Connecticut, fifty miles north. "It's safer there. Nice people," he said. Kitty might even find a nice fellow to marry there.

Kitty said no. "I can't go." She couldn't imagine living in the suburbs. "I feel free in New York," she said. "I'm alive here." She told her parents she could find a job in a safe neighborhood. She'd stay in touch by phone and take the train up to New Canaan for regular visits. And she won them over. Kitty stayed in the city. At first she bunked in an extra room in her grandfather's apartment. She worked as a secretary at an insurance company, earning enough to rent an apartment of her own. It was 1954, the year of the Army-McCarthy hearings on television, Bill Haley and His Comets' "Rock around the Clock" on the radio. Kitty worked as a secretary, then as a waitress, then as a hostess in an Italian restaurant. Later she tried tending bar at a pub in Hollis, Queens, the kind of neighborhood joint that had Christmas lights around the bar mirror all year. She made good money tending bar—tax free. She made friends. In time she took over as the bar's manager, often working two shifts a day. Kitty settled in Queens, statistically the safest of the city's five boroughs. And sure enough, she fell in love.

2

Opposites

"It was such a time," Mary Ann Zielonko says. "Such a time to be alive."

Mary Ann was twenty-four in the spring of 1963. Sharp-witted and gifted with what TV and radio commercials called vim, she was blonde and pretty—people said she had movie-star looks. Smart too. After acing an employment test, Mary Ann went to work as a Teletype operator for Western Union, feeding terse, ALL-CAPS dispatches into a humming console that was part typewriter, part prototype fax machine. Many of the messages she had typed over the previous winter featured the words KENNEDY, KHRUSHCHEV, and CRISIS. After the USSR moved atomic missiles into Cuba in October 1962 and President Kennedy called Soviet premier Nikita Khrushchev's bluff by imposing a naval blockade, the world spent two weeks wobbling over what Khrushchev described as "the abyss of a world nuclear-missile war." Eight months earlier, Americans had watched the skies for a trace of astronaut John Glenn's Mercury capsule, *Friendship 7.* Now they worried that every shooting star or passing plane might bring the end of history. "People today act like it's overdramatic to say we thought the world might blow up any minute," Mary Ann says. "But they weren't there, were they?"

Dark, briny lower Manhattan could hardly have been more different from today's gleaming downtown. At Washington Market in what is now Tribeca, old-timers hawked vegetables and fruits, pork and partridges, following the age-old tradition of quoting prices in English shillings, twelve and a half cents per shilling. Farther south, merchants at the gull-swarmed Fulton Fish Market in the shadow of the Brooklyn Bridge sold five hundred tons of seafood on a banner day—a million pounds of Gulf Coast shrimp, Maine lobster, king crab from Alaska, sturgeon and cod from Nova Scotia—a daily haul totaling twenty kinds of shellfish, thirty-five species of freshwater fish, and more than 130 varieties of saltwater fish. Each night after closing time the local gulls, rats, pigeons, and stray cats and dogs fought over the skins, heads, and guts the fishmongers threw out.

Twenty blocks from the fish market, twenty-four-year-old Mary Ann passed basements and subway stops marked with black-and-yellow FALLOUT SHELTER signs on her way to Western Union headquarters, a brick tower on Hudson Street. She felt a little safer every day the world didn't blow up. After the Cuban Missile Crisis, the threat of instant thermonuclear extinction gave way to the Cold War, a chronic condition that made a lower-level threat feel as routine as the weather report: *Partly cloudy with a slight chance of atomic attack.*

The speed of life was quickening. Want progress? In 1963, the year atomic isotopes from H-bomb tests began showing up in the enamel of schoolchildren's teeth, New York's Consolidated Edison announced plans to build a million-kilowatt nuclear power plant in the middle of Queens. The city tore down Pennsylvania Station to make way for a renovated Madison Square Garden. The newest TV sets showed programs in color! Want culture? George C. Scott was playing Shylock outdoors in producer Joe Papp's brand-new Shakespeare in the Park while Zero Mostel tickled Broadway crowds in *A Funny Thing Happened on the Way to the Forum* and Brooklyn's twenty-year-old Barbra Streisand, fresh off her star-making Broadway debut in *I Can Get It for You Wholesale*, had her first hit record. Andy Warhol unveiled his silkscreens of soup cans and celebrities at his Factory, a converted ConEd station on Forty-Seventh Street, where Tennessee Williams and Norman Mailer rubbed elbows with Liz Taylor, Marilyn Monroe, and Factory "superstars" (Warhol invented the term) Ultra Violet and Taylor Mead at showings of such films as *Handjob, Blowjob,* and a feature-length study titled *Taylor Mead's Ass.* Twelve blocks away, Gloria Steinem donned satin rabbit ears to work undercover at the new Playboy Club on Fifty-Ninth Street, enduring long nights of cottontail-pinching for her magazine exposé "I Was a Playboy Bunny."

Mary Ann found a different scene fifty blocks south of the Playboy Club. "Greenwich Village was the one place where I felt like I belonged," she recalls. The capital of American bohemia had called to Mary Ann since the day she picked up a paperback novel in a bookshop in Merrimack, New Hampshire. She was fifteen years old and the book was *The Price of Salt,* a lesbian romance by Patricia Highsmith, writing as "Claire Morgan." *The Price of Salt* suggested to Mary Ann that there were other people like her, girls who liked girls. She moved on to gaily lurid pulp. *Women's Barracks. The Third Sex. No Adam for Eve.* Pulp authors of the time ducked government censorship by teaching their Sapphic characters a hard lesson: in the end, lesbian characters could turn "normal," go mad, or die. Still such novels found loyal readers who thrilled to the sin that preceded the payoff.

Even at fifteen, Mary Ann knew she wasn't cut out to be anybody's housewife. "I was a misfit. At least in New Hampshire." Pulp novels offered glimpses of a place her favorite pulp author, Ann Bannon, described as "Emerald City, Wonderland, and Brigadoon combined— a place where gay people could walk the crooked streets hand in hand." As Bannon's streetwise heroine Beebo Brinker told a new arrival, "That's all the Village is, honey, just one crazy little soap opera after another, one piled on top of the next, *ad infinitum.* Mary loves Jane loves Joan loves Jean loves Beebo. . . . It goes on forever."

Mary Ann was sixteen when she left New Hampshire for Greenwich Village. "My mother was glad to see me go." She found work as a file clerk and loved the city from the start. Manhattan's grid pulsed with life: traffic and traffic cops, pedestrians and parades, even the occasional circus act passing by practically unnoticed. You know you're in New York when a team of twenty circus elephants plods down Sixth Avenue and hardly anybody stops to watch. It made quite a sight: a few tourists gaping and pointing, while the rest of the pedestrians hurry by. The only New Yorkers who seemed to notice the spectacle on Sixth Avenue were cabbies honking their horns at the elephants.

Much of the city was stacked with office towers and tenements, but the smoky, neon-lit Village was different. The difference was attributed to the geology of Manhattan Island. Ancient bedrock was said to rise almost to street level under midtown and lower Manhattan. A sparkly mica schist called Manhattan schist, solid enough to hold up skyscrapers, the bedrock burst through the surface all over the city. It was the black rock that children clamber up and down in Central Park. But this schist was supposedly absent between midtown and Canal Street, leaving a subterranean trough where bedrock ran deeper. Above it, centuries of New York lives filled the soft trough with layer upon layer of coal ash and table scraps, oyster and clam shells, pottery, bricks and glass, fish and dog and cat and rat bones, horse skeletons, driftwood, shingles, shoes, newspaper pulp, and a thousand other ingredients of Manhattan's middens. Such landfill wasn't thought to be dense enough to support tall buildings. The squishy sediment laid down by the city's past lives could barely support the low-rise brownstones of the Village—or so went the geological line of thinking until half a century later, when a Rutgers University professor used core samples to demonstrate that "the Manhattan bedrock myth" was an urban legend. Plausible, memorable, but false. Solid schist actually lies just under the surface in the blocks between Canal Street and midtown. In all likelihood that area became a trough in the skyline for economic reasons: few builders saw a need for office space in the Village and its environs, home to the squalid, violent Five Points slums and later the factories of Soho, and still later the beatniks, folkies, and "sexual deviates" who made the Village a place where Mary Ann found "like-minded people. Girls like me. Girls who liked me."

In the eyes of the law, they were criminals. Homosexuality was illegal in 1963 under the sodomy laws of every state but Illinois, and even in Illinois gay men and lesbians demanding their rights risked arrest for disorderly conduct or public lewdness. San Francisco police busted gay bars and heads on Castro Street. New York's vice squads made a hobby of raiding clubs like the Swing Rendezvous on MacDougal Street, where the crowd was mostly female. A girl bar, cops called the place, or a girl-girl bar. Sometimes they used uglier names. "It wasn't a gay bar because we weren't 'gay' yet," Mary Ann says today. "If you liked women, you were a lesbian, and if you were a lesbian, you didn't go around proud of it. You were careful. Because there were people who would beat you up if they knew."

The Swing Rendezvous was an underground club at 117 MacDougal. The Swing had a long wooden bar scored with more initials than a grade-school desk, vinyl platters playing on the PA, multicolored scrims shading the lightbulbs overhead, women of all shapes and sizes crowding the dance floor. The dancers wore Shalimar, Arpège, and L'Aimant. They slow-danced to Piaf, Judy Garland, and Streisand's "Cry Me a River." Some slow-danced even when the music changed and everybody else started doing the Twist or the Swim.

One night Mary Ann was making her way through the fragrant crowd to the bar when a cute brunette appeared at her elbow, a girl she hadn't seen before. Pegged slacks, a loose blouse, dark tousled hair. "Don't I know you from somewhere?" the girl asked.

Mary Ann had heard better pickup lines. "I don't think so."

Kitty Genovese smiled. "Oh, I think I do," she said. "I'm Kitty."

They danced, the pretty blonde and her new partner, drawing appreciative glances. "Kitty was a good dancer. People noticed her," Mary Ann recalls. After a dance they stood at the bar, chatting, Mary Ann sipping a Rolling Rock while Kitty ordered a cocktail. Other women watched Kitty, who kept her eyes on Mary Ann. Until Kitty slipped into the crowd. "I lost her. She must have gone to the ladies' room or something," Mary Ann says. Scanning the club, she realized that she didn't know Kitty's last name. Never got her number. Had she told Kitty her own name? Or where she lived? She wasn't sure. "I thought I might never see her again."

Mary Ann rode the IRT subway uptown to Seventy-Second and Broadway. She was renting a room at a boardinghouse on Seventy-Fourth Street, twenty dollars a week for a bed, a closet, and a window overlooking a brick wall. No phone, no meals, no pets, and no news of Kitty as three days and nights passed. Then it was St. Patrick's Day.

March 17, 1963: New York's "Fighting Sixty-Ninth" infantry regiment and its team of Irish wolfhounds led ranks of kilted bagpipers, police- and fire-department marching bands, and open cars laden with dignitaries, including Mayor Robert Wagner, past St. Patrick's Cathedral. The parade music carried north and west to the boardinghouse where Mary Ann came home from work to find a note tacked to her door.

I'll call you at 7. The phone across the street.

"I knew it was her," Mary Ann says.

A phone booth stood at the northwest corner of Seventy-Fourth and Broadway, behind the Ansonia Hotel. Mary Ann had a rich aunt who lived at the grand, gargoyled Ansonia. The aunt had invited her over for tea exactly once since Mary Ann moved into the no-frills boardinghouse across the street. The Ansonia, like the aunt, was thirty-five years past its Roaring Twenties prime, a time when live seals splashed in a lobby fountain while Enrico Caruso practiced vocal scales in his apartment upstairs. Another resident, opera buff Babe Ruth, liked to syncopate the great Caruso's practice by rolling baseballs down the stairs. A rooftop farm produced fresh eggs for residents and guests. The Bambino drove a Stutz Bearcat—sometimes on the sidewalk—honking at pedestrians, stopping to sign autographs for cops who pulled him over. Tallulah Bankhead was known to step out of the Ansonia and hail a taxi by revealing that she was naked under her fur coat. Mary Ann seemed to be having the opposite effect on traffic in 1963, dodging Dodges, finned Fords, Volkswagen bugs, and chunky yellow cabs that sped up as she picked her way across Broadway to a pay phone that was already ringing.

"Hello?"

"It's me." Kitty's breathy voice. "Where can we meet?"

"The Seven Steps," Mary Ann said. "Do you know it?"

"I'll find it."

An underground bar that welcomed butches and femmes of both sexes, the Seven Steps was "secretly famous," one patron wrote years later. "Erroll Flynn used to drop in. He loved to do poppers and always had some on him. Audrey Hepburn visited. Also Jack and Jackie Kennedy when he was a senator from Massachusetts." Mary Ann nodded to Mitch the bartender as she entered the Seven Steps that night. Mitch was about thirty, six feet tall, and female. Tough enough to talk back to vice cops, toss out the occasional tourist who came in to ogle the freaks in their habitat, and to fight off a mugger who jumped her one night as she closed up. Mitch would be dead in a year, lying in a stairwell under a bloodstained topcoat. But tonight she was looking sharp in a suit and black tie. Her bartending outfit was a crime: crossdressing was against the law. She plopped a Rolling Rock on the bar for Mary Ann, a green bottle for St. Paddy's Day. "Hello, girl."

"Have you seen . . . ?"

Mitch knew who she meant. "Not yet."

Mary Ann watched the door while she sipped her beer. She finished one beer and asked for another. Finally Kitty came through the door. Moving between dancers, many of them half a head taller than she was, she gave no sign of seeing Mary Ann until she was close enough to touch. Then she looked right at her.

Fifty years later, Mary Ann recalls that moment as the best of her life. "Sometimes you meet a person and you just *know*."

"Hi," Kitty said, and it sounded like an invitation.

They ordered a round and got acquainted again, leaning close to hear each other over the music. "Kitty was Italian American, I'm Polish American. She was Catholic, I was agnostic. She was so . . . charismatic, and I'm a quiet person," Mary Ann says. "Opposites attract, you know?"

The boardinghouse was dark when they arrived long after midnight. Mary Ann's nosy landlady had gone to bed. Mary Ann led Kitty upstairs to her room. Their first night together was the first of three hundred and sixty. By morning they knew they wanted to live together.

Kitty was twenty-seven. Mary Ann was twenty-four. Kitty managed a bar in Queens, twenty minutes east of Manhattan. The two of them spent two happy weeks in a motel room near the bar "but that's not real life," Mary Ann says. "Kitty was happy, but it made me nervous. I didn't think it was safe. Who lives in a motel?" They searched apartment ads and found a one-bedroom on Austin Street in Kew Gardens, next door to the Long Island Rail Road station.

It was a second-floor flat, the kind New Yorkers call a taxpayer. Kitty and Mary Ann's apartment was one of fourteen similar units in a two-story building that typified the neighborhood, a faux-Tudor with crossbeams showing on the whitewashed façade and chimney pots on the shingled roof. There were storefronts on the ground floor, apartments upstairs. Thirty-foot oaks shaded the curb out front, where drivers jockeyed for parking spots on Austin Street. There was never enough parking. Double-parked businessmen ran their jackets and dress shirts into Better Way French Cleaners, where a sign announced that the place now boasted a CLEANOMAT, where young mothers took turns at shiny white coin-operated washers and dryers. Next door, the Austin Book Shop stocked the Cold War thrillers *Fail-Safe* and *Seven Days in May* as well as James Baldwin's *The Fire Next Time*, Rachel Carson's *Silent Spring*, Steinbeck's *Travels with Charley*, and a new Charlie Brown book, *Happiness Is a Warm Puppy*. At the TV-radio shop beside Regent Wine and Liquor, teenagers pawed through 45-rpm records looking for the Rooftop Singers' bouncy "Walk Right In" and the Beach Boys' number-one "Surfin' USA." Franken's Pharmacy on the corner stocked Absorbine Jr., Coppertone, Epsom salts, nickel popsicles, and Marvel comics including the first issue of *The Amazing Spider-Man*, published that very week (cover price twelve cents, 2014 value $40,000).

At the building's southeast end, opposite the drugstore, stood Bailey's Pub, open most nights until 4:00 a.m. Bailey's wasn't the neighbors' favorite establishment. Music and late-night arguments sometimes spilled through the tavern's double doors, waking residents in the rest of the Tudor building and in the Mowbray Apartments across the street, Kew Gardens' tallest building. Some of the fights outside Bailey's were marital spats. Most amounted to nothing more than shouting matches, but a few escalated into slaps or punches. The neighbors learned to look the other way. Even if you didn't think a man had a right to give his woman a smack, try stopping him, they told themselves. Likely as not they'd both turn on you and chase you down the sidewalk.

Aside from Bailey's, Kew Gardens was peace itself. There hadn't been a murder in the neighborhood in years. Homeowners left their doors unlocked. Parents thought nothing of sending their daughters out alone after dark to sell Girl Scout cookies. "It is one of the better neighborhoods," a beat cop reported. "There are few crimes. You only get the usual complaints about boys playing or garbage cans being turned over."

Tony Corrado ran a furniture shop on Austin Street. In March 1963 a peppy brunette tapped on his door. "That was my introduction to Kitty," Corrado recalled. She asked him to reupholster a used sofa-bed for her. When the job was done, Corrado and his son Billy carried the sofa-bed upstairs for her.

"Yeah—right in here," she said, leading them to a door in back of the Tudor building, the side facing the railroad tracks. Kitty hadn't bought the sofa-bed from Corrado; she'd just given him a few dollars to patch it up. Still he was glad to help her out. "Kitty had that effect on people," recalls Billy Corrado. "She was supernice, with a smile for everybody." People wanted to help her out if only to see that smile. Teenager Billy, who hoped to become a priest, lugged her sofa-bed up the stairs while trying not to notice how pretty Kitty was. He figured the local boys would develop crushes on the new girl on the block.

His father figured Kitty and her blonde-headed roommate would liven up the neighborhood. "I thought they were airline stewardesses," Tony Corrado recalled. "I said, 'Boy, there's going to be a lot of wild parties up here!'" Kew Gardens, halfway between the city's two airports, LaGuardia and Idlewild, was home to several flight attendants and even a few pilots. Still the place was "pretty boring," Corrado warned Kitty. "Nothing ever happens around here."

Kitty and Mary Ann set up house at the top of the stairs. Kitty wanted a homey place, while Mary Ann's tastes were more bohemian. Their apartment was a compromise: cozy enough for Kitty with its kitchenette, throw rugs, and flower box, with contemporary touches to suit her roommate. Their five-sided living room, shaped like half a Stop sign, held the sofa-bed, a coffee table, and bookcases full of records as well as books, a stereo, a radio sitting on a windowsill, and an easel placed near the window, where the light was best. Mary Ann, who was taking lessons from a Kew Gardens artist, hung one of her canvases, a female nude, on the living room wall.

Neither roommate had the least interest in growing flowers, so the flower box filled up with records and books. Mary Ann liked fiction and poetry, from Hart Crane, James Agee, and T. S. Eliot to the lesbian pulp of her formative years, while Kitty preferred nonfiction, from President Kennedy's *Profiles in Courage* to Betty Friedan's *Feminine Mystique*, with its odd mix of proto-feminism and homophobia. Friedan urged woman to throw off their shackles if not yet their bras, but while her New Woman could be a doctor, lawyer, or chief executive, she wasn't supposed to be gay. Friedan described lesbians as "the lavender menace."

Kitty read her anyway. "I like what's real," she told Mary Ann. Nonfiction was real. The newspapers were real.

Mary Ann told her that fiction had its own reality. It was like the difference between painting and photography. Which is truer? Mary Ann didn't claim to know, but she preferred the former. She told

Kitty that she wanted to paint her, but wasn't sure she was ready yet. She wasn't sure she was good enough yet. Kitty liked that—not just that Mary Ann wanted to paint her; she liked the idea that Mary Ann wanted to get better before she tried painting her lover.

They discussed art, music, movies, astrology. "We were both Cancers," Mary Ann says. According to a horoscope Kitty read in a newspaper, that made them compatible. "*Cancer and Cancer, a very romantic match . . .*," she said.

"That's us," Mary Ann said.

"*. . . intensely emotional, highly sexual. And jealous!*"

Mary Ann didn't want to be jealous, but she couldn't help noticing how people looked at Kitty. Tony Corrado couldn't wait to carry her sofa-bed up the stairs. One of Kitty's ex-lovers kept coming around for months after they broke up. "Just to be friends," the girl said, making eyes at Kitty, who was more flirtatious than Mary Ann, more sociable, a little coquettish when it suited her, batting her eyes at people who couldn't wait to buy her a drink. Mary Ann called her on it: "You're leading them on."

Kitty said she was just being friendly. "Anyway, you've got nothing to worry about. I'm going home with you."

Mary Ann got sick of commuting between their apartment in Queens and the Western Union building in Manhattan. She wanted to spend more time with Kitty. "I'm quitting my job," she said.

"Okay," Kitty said. "What else can you do?"

"I'm good with numbers," Mary Ann said. "But I'd rather paint."

Kitty rolled her eyes. "That's a lot of help." She asked around and found Mary Ann a bartending job at Club Chris, ten minutes from their apartment. Kitty had to swear that her "friend" was a veteran mixologist.

"I'd never been behind a bar, never mixed a martini," Mary Ann recalls, "but I asked myself, 'How hard can it be?'"

3

Garden Suburb

Kitty tended bar at Ev's 11th Hour, a neighborhood tavern on Jamaica Boulevard in Hollis, Queens. When people asked what she did for a living she always said, "I'm a barmaid." But she was smart and reliable, and before long she was managing the place for the absentee owner. That meant double shifts. After working for twelve to fifteen hours, she'd help the late-shift bartender close up and then drive home after three in the morning. It was a ten-minute drive from Ev's to Kew Gardens and the apartment she shared with Mary Ann. On most nights every parking space within three blocks of their building would be taken at that hour, so she parked in the lot at the Long Island Rail Road station, ignoring the NO PARKING signs. The cops never ticketed cars in the L.I.R.R. lot. By that time the ground-floor shops on Austin Street had been closed for hours. Bailey's Pub at the end of the block might be open, humming with jukebox music until three-thirty or four, except on slow nights, when the manager closed up a little early. On those nights the sidewalk was deserted, the block so quiet Kitty could hear her footsteps.

Around three-thirty a bus rolled through the intersection of Austin Street and Lefferts Boulevard: the nearly empty Q10, spilling yellow light.

Kitty walked past the Interlude Coffee House to a door in back of her building. She let herself in and climbed a narrow flight of stairs. All quiet on the second-floor landing. The Farrars, her neighbors across the hall, were early-to-bed people who turned in before the end of the Johnny Carson show. During the days, Sophie Farrar would go into Kitty and Mary Ann's unlocked apartment if she heard the phone ringing, and take messages for them. That's the kind of block it was. Neighbors helped each other out. Sophie and Joe Farrar would be awake in three and a half hours, Joe poking his head out to pick up the morning paper, Sophie making coffee. Sometimes when Kitty couldn't sleep she'd stay up, join Sophie for coffee and then drive the Farrars' kids to school.

Kitty let herself in. She opened and shut the door with barely a click to keep from waking Mary Ann. The apartment smelled of paint and turpentine. Mary Ann had been giving the place a coat of tan paint. Kitty peeled off her work clothes and slipped into bed beside her. Kew Gardens was quiet until the next train rushed by, rattling the window and the walls.

Their part of Queens had been farmland until the railroad hooked it to Manhattan, nine miles to the west. In the mid-nineteenth century the spot of land that would become Kew Gardens was a two- to three-hour trek from Manhattan: a ferry ride across the East River followed by those nine dusty, axle-rattling miles in a horse-drawn buggy wending through corn and onion fields, vineyards, and apple orchards. Local farmers raised goats, chickens, turkeys, ducks, pigeons, shaggy Cotswold sheep, hogs, and honeybees. They stocked city-bound wagons with the apples, meat, and eggs that helped worried New Yorkers survive the Civil War. A ban on burials in lower Manhattan, where real estate was getting too precious to spend on graveyards, led to a cemetery boom in Brooklyn and Queens. Brooklyn's four-hundred-acre Green-Wood Cemetery became a tourist attraction with its lakes, rolling hills, monuments, and double-deck mausoleums (some with Tiffany windows) engraved with famous names including that of Louis Comfort Tiffany. "It is the ambition of the New Yorker to live upon the Fifth Avenue," the *New York Times* claimed in 1866, "to take his airings in the Park, and to sleep with his fathers in Green-Wood." Samuel F. B. Morse was buried there, along with sewing-machine inventor Elias Howe, F. A. O. Schwarz, and more than two hundred thousand others including William "Boss" Tweed, who sailed seven thousand miles to reach his final destination. Jailed for fraud and embezzlement in 1875, the Tammany Hall kingpin escaped, fled to Spain, and signed on as a sailor—the goutiest, ruddiest three-hundred-pound seaman in King Alfonso XIII's merchant fleet. He might have lived *felizmente* ever after if not for Spanish newspaper readers who recognized Boss Tweed from Thomas Nast's famed political cartoons. They pointed him out to American sailors, who shanghaied Tweed and took him home. He died in jail and was buried at Green-Wood, one more Manhattanite laid to rest in the cheaper land across the East River.

Queens's Calvary Cemetery was even bigger and busier than Green-Wood. Soon after the Catholic necropolis opened its gates in 1848, one account tallied "fifty burials a day, half of them poor Irish under seven years of age." By 1900 its seven hundred thousand residents made Calvary the most populous cemetery in America. Today, with more than three million, it still holds the title.

Maple Grove Cemetery, farther east, was a country churchyard by comparison. Still it spurred the growth of the village that became Kew Gardens. With more than eighty thousand plots by the 1870s, the cemetery held more than ten times as many people as the village around it. In 1875 the Long Island Rail Road built a station in central Queens to accommodate mourners riding steam-powered trains to Maple Grove. The station was called Hopedale. When it was modernized twenty years later, New York City police commissioner Theodore Roosevelt presided over opening ceremonies. Standing in front of a station house festooned with the forty-four-starred American flag, the bespectacled future president declared that he was bullish on Queens County and invited New Yorkers to visit Queens's peaceable acres and newly cobbled, tree-lined boulevards.

Three years later, in 1898, Queens joined Manhattan, Brooklyn, the Bronx, and Staten Island in a new, five-borough New York City, the most populous city in the Western Hemisphere. In all the world, only London's population of six million surpassed New York's 3.1 million. In those days the Richmond Hill Country Club's golf course ran through the middle of the borough. Its stately clubhouse stood on a hill overlooking spring-fed Crystal Lake. A hundred and seventy feet above sea level, the clubhouse, designed by Henry Beaumont Herts and Hugh Tallant, builders of Broadway theaters and the Brooklyn Academy of Music, was the highest point in Queens. From its roof you could see Manhattan's new "sky-scraper," the twenty-two-story Flatiron Building, rising ten miles to the west. At least you could see to Manhattan until 1910, when the clubhouse moved downhill. That was the year the Long Island Rail Road electrified its Main Line from Pennsylvania Station. Suddenly the middle of Queens wasn't two hours or even half an hour from midtown Manhattan; it was sixteen minutes on the new century's version of a bullet train. Central Queens was suddenly as reachable from Penn Station as City Hall or Harlem. Almost overnight, land near the Long Island Rail Road station became too precious to waste on fairways and tennis courts. Workmen tore down the clubhouse, carted the pieces down-hill, and put Herts and Tallant's clubhouse back together half a mile away. Engineers plugged the underground spring that fed Crystal Lake. They drained the lake. Horse and mule teams plowed the area's rich soil into the lake bed, leveling the land for another new railroad station: the Kew Gardens station, named by railroad executives to suggest the petaled tranquility of England's renowned botanical gardens in Kew, near London. Leave it to businessmen to drain a lake, turn it into a train station strewn with gravel and wires, and call it a garden.

K ew Gardens was and is the smallest town in Queens. Wedged between Forest Hills and Richmond Hill, the suburban village comprises seven north-south blocks and eight east-west blocks, a total of fifty-six city blocks, less than one square mile. After the crime, many Americans would picture Kew Gardens as a New York neighborhood like Hell's Kitchen at its most hellish, a forbidding cityscape of fire escapes and alleys strewn with trash. The real Kew Gardens was a leafy middle-class retreat for machinists, nurses, schoolteachers, tailors, upholsterers, railroad and restaurant workers, butchers, barbers, bartenders, and the occasional music-maker who took the train to Broadway or Carnegie Hall. Strangers greeted each other with a "Good morning" or a "Hello, neighbor."

F. Scott Fitzgerald was among the Manhattanites who sped

through the Kew Gardens commuter-rail station en route to coastal retreats on Long Island. To the north Fitzgerald and other passengers saw mountains of cinders and trash at the Corona ash dump, where workmen emptied wagonloads of coal ash as well as tons of garbage, horse manure, and dead animals from all over the city, day after day, year after year, until the dump loomed over its surroundings. In *The Great Gatsby*, Fitzgerald named it the Valley of Ashes, "a fantastic farm where ashes grow like wheat into ridges and hills and grotesque gardens; where ashes take the form of houses and chimneys and rising smoke." This was the wasteland between neon Manhattan and golden West Egg, the grubby purgatory where Daisy Buchanan ran over her husband's lover without bothering to stop, sealing Gatsby's doom. But others looked just down the road from Corona's ash heaps and saw the future.

According to Queens historian Barry Lewis, the leafy village that sprouted around the Kew Gardens rail station appealed to "a cosmopolitan generation that wanted the culture and opportunities the city offered but not the nerve-wracking assault on the senses and demeaning lack of personal space that came with urban territory." Forty years before so-called father of suburbia William Levitt built his protean suburb, Levittown, fifteen miles farther out on Long Island, Kew Gardens was what Lewis called "the perfect garden suburb." The next village to the east, not quite as nice, was called Utopia.

During the Roaring Twenties, before filmmakers moved almost all their operations to southern California, Queens still served as the movies' East Coast capital. Charlie Chaplin lived in Kew Gardens, riding the train to Astoria Studios from his Arts and Crafts cottage two blocks from the station where Kitty Genovese would park her car forty years later. Will Rogers and his wife, Betty, raised four children in a bungalow nearby. Dorothy Parker, Anaïs Nin, and George Gershwin rode the train between Manhattan and their Kew

Gardens homes. Gershwin sometimes annoyed other passengers with his whistling. One can only imagine hearing him whistle the first few bars of "Rhapsody in Blue" during his commute. An avid tennis player, he spent leisure hours on the local courts. In winter, when the courts were flooded and frozen for ice-skating, Gershwin skated figure eights. In later years the ice would be etched by neighborhood youngsters including Burt Bacharach, Paul Simon, and Jerry Springer. By then, Fitzgerald's Valley of Ashes had been cleared and drained by city planner Robert Moses, who turned the Corona dump—future site of the National Tennis Center and the Mets' Citi Field—into parkland for the 1939–'40 New York World's Fair. Now it was the garden suburb that was showing signs of decay. The celebrities had moved away, their houses and luxury apartments divided into duplexes and one- or two-bedroom flats inhabited by strivers like upholsterer Tony Corrado, railroad worker Joe Farrar, and "misfits" like Kitty and Mary Ann. Kew Gardens was changing.

The train station was still its hub, and the Mowbray building on Austin Street was the closest Kew Gardens had to a skyscraper. An aging pile a hundred feet high, the Mowbray had been Queens' answer to the Ansonia when it opened its brass-and-glass doors in 1924. Its Roaring Twenties residents enjoyed maid service, room service, a roof garden, and dances in air-conditioned ballrooms. All that was a dim memory by 1963. Rents fell as forty years of pigeon droppings eroded the stone around the tower's arched windows. Paint peeled in the Mowbray's once-grand apartments.

Commuters riding east from Penn Station sped under the East River, emerged on aboveground tracks in Queens—into sunlight—passed warehouses and apartment blocks hung with fire escapes and laundry until, fifteen minutes or so later, the train pulled up behind the Tudor building where Kitty and Mary Ann lived, across Austin Street from the Mowbray. If you stepped onto the platform there, you might not be impressed by the neighborhood, but you wouldn't be worried. You wouldn't look over your shoulder and move your wallet to a front pocket.

"Not a tough neighborhood," recalled Jacob Cohen, who grew up in the same Tudor apartment building Mary Ann and Kitty moved into in 1963. Young Jacob had moved out by then, but the block hadn't changed since he was filching candy from the corner drugstore, sneaking into Bailey's Pub, and sleeping through the roar of trains going by his bedroom window. When Jacob was eighteen, he noticed that there weren't many cabs at the Kew Gardens station, particularly late at night, so he'd park there in his rusty, tubercular Ford, waiting for trains coming east from Penn Station. "I'd offer to drive the people home. I'd tell them, 'Pay me whatever you think is fair.'" Cohen's late-night fares helped pay his mother's rent. Finally he got out of town—drove to the Catskills, landed a gig as a standup comic, and changed his name from Jake Cohen to Rodney Dangerfield. He joked onstage about his boyhood in Kew Gardens.

"Not a tough neighborhood," Dangerfield said. "I mean, one night a guy pulls a knife on me. But it wasn't a real professional job—it was a butter knife."

A knifing in Kew Gardens was so unlikely that it sounded like a joke.

4

Tigers and Ants

The slender man at the end of the bar could nurse a beer for an hour. Kitty or Mary Ann may have served him a few times without really noticing the light-skinned Negro hunched over his beer, a watchful man with wide-set eyes, his features tapering to a sparse goatee on his pointy chin. People said he resembled a cat.

Winston Moseley was twenty-eight years old in 1963, the same age as Kitty. Intelligence tests he took a year later would put his IQ at 135. He worked at Raygram, a business-machine company in Mount Vernon, the town just north of the Bronx, punching data cards for the company's first-generation Remington Rand computers. After work he drove home to his wife, Betty, their two boys, and five German shepherds in South Ozone Park, Queens, a wedge of land between Aqueduct Racetrack and Idlewild Airport. No part of Queens was growing faster as the borough's population pushed two million. If Queens had been an independent city it would have been the nation's fifth largest, ahead of Detroit and just behind Philadelphia. Children skipped rope and biked on South Ozone Park's breezy streets. Their parents pushed lawn mowers and tended flower beds on tidy front lawns. Seagulls wheeled among the Eastern Airlines DC-8s and TWA and Pan Am 707s going to and from the airport's runways. Some takeoffs and landings shook the aluminum tiles of Moseley's four-bedroom house on Sutter Avenue the way trains shook the Tudor building in Kew Gardens, ten minutes away.

Moseley could make it home from work by six or six fifteen, depending on traffic, but sometimes he decided to stop at a bar for a beer or two. Why rush? Betty could feed the dogs and the kids. A beer might relax him, and he needed to relax. Let it get a little later. Otherwise this might be one of those sleepless nights when he slipped out of bed at two or three in the morning and went for a drive.

He had taken a bumpy road to this barstool. Born at Harlem Hospital late in the winter of 1935, Winston grew up as an only child in a walk-up apartment on West 147th Street. His mother, Fannie, and her husband, Alphonso, battled fleas in the summer, roaches and mice and each other all year. Fannie Moseley, from Flint, Michigan, could outtalk an auctioneer. She bullied Alphonso, a harried-looking native of Selma, Alabama, who had begun a career of petty crime with a long-ago joyride in a Model-T Ford. Alphonso learned to play guitar in a boys' reformatory. He joined a dance band, toured the Midwest, and met Fannie while playing a gig in Flint. They married in 1934 despite his suspicions that Fannie had other lovers. They moved to New York, where Alphonso found a job as a subway change-booth clerk. Winston, their only child, was born on March 2, 1935. His boyhood was "blissful"—Fannie's word—with his mother noting his every bowel movement, boasting that her Winston was toilet-trained at the age of four months. He could read before he entered the first grade. Fannie indulged his interests in painting, poetry, and music—he played the flute—but sometimes left him alone all night while Alphonso worked in the change booth and she slept with other men.

One day Fannie told nine-year-old Winston that she had a growth in her belly. Not a little brother or sister for him. "A tumor. A cancer," she said. "The doctor's got to cut it out of me." Fannie went to the hospital and never came home. But not because she died. As Winston learned later, his mother was sick all right: sick of her husband, sick of living in Harlem with the two of them. She went to the hospital, then fled home to Michigan.

Alphonso couldn't raise the boy himself, not while he worked nights in the subway. He shipped Winston to a farm in Holly, Michigan, an hour from Detroit, to live with Fannie's mother. Instead of playing stickball and riding the subway, Winston found himself wandering corn and bean fields. He gathered eggs, learned to milk a cow, watched sheep and hogs being born and slaughtered, and discovered the Detroit Tigers.

Led by first baseman Hank Greenberg, the Tigers spent the summer and fall of 1945 battling the Washington Senators for the American League pennant. Strapping, sad-eyed Greenberg had missed four and a half seasons while serving in the Army, the longest World War II hitch of any big-league player. He hit a home run in his first game back, homered again on the August weekend that the B-29 *Enola Gay* dropped an atom bomb on Hiroshima, and stepped to the plate on the season's final day with the pennant on the line. The Tigers trailed the St. Louis Browns, 3–2, in the ninth inning. The bases were loaded, the sun dipping behind the stands, fans squinting to follow the action. There were no lights at Sportsman's Park in St. Louis. Umpire George Pipgras said, "Sorry, Hank. I'm going to call the game. I can't see the baseball."

Greenberg said, "Don't worry, George. I can see it fine." He slugged the next pitch for a pennant-winning grand slam. The Tigers went on to beat the Chicago Cubs in the 1945 World Series, capping a thrilling season for fans, including a lonely ten-year-old boy spending his first fall in Michigan.

The following summer, Greenberg and the '46 Tigers chased Ted Williams's Boston Red Sox. With Jackie Robinson still in the minors, a year from breaking baseball's color line, Detroit's so-called Hebrew Hammer appealed to an outsider like Winston. A native New Yorker, Greenberg had dreamed of signing with the Yankees, but they had Lou Gehrig at first base, so Greenberg wound up in Detroit, where he spent his rookie year pining for home, missing his mother back in the Bronx.

Seventeen years later, sipping foam off the top of a fifty-cent beer, Winston Moseley had time to reflect on his Michigan years. There was more to remember than Hank Greenberg's heroics. It was during those days on his grandmother's farm that Winston learned about barnyard animals and insects. The sex habits of dogs, hogs, chickens, and ducks intrigued him. (The drake sometimes drowns the duck during mating.) "I intend to be a scientist," he wrote in a grade-school essay. "I intend to go to college for a long time. If I don't become a scientist I will be a special agent for the F.B.I. Someday I might even be famous." Meanwhile he admired the cunning of crows and the tireless teamwork of ants. He read every book he could find on animals, particularly insects. He knew that while most people call all insects "bugs," only a few species with penetrating, sucking beaks are true bugs. He knew that roaches, which are not bugs, enjoy nothing more than packing into small spaces together, feeling each others' bodies against their backs and stomachs, snug as bugs in rugs. They felt safer that way. Other people might cringe at the thought of insects' lives because insects are so different from us, so alien, but Winston liked that about them. They weren't like people. They were more like perfect little machines, reacting to light, heat, or scent without thinking. He wondered how it felt to be an ant.

When Winston was ten, Alphonso moved to Detroit and sent for him. "I love you, boy," Alphonso said. He built Winston his first ant farm by replacing a secondhand aquarium's side panels with inch-wide strips of clear plastic. The boy spent hours watching his red harvester ants digging tunnels, sharing food, feeding and cleaning their giant-bellied queen, caring for their young. He liked other insects too: grasshoppers catapulting themselves over sidewalks, honeybees working themselves to death, fireflies signaling potential mates by blinking the cold yellow-green light in their bellies—luciferin, the chemical was called. Ants were his favorites, though. Something about the relentless way they worked, and sometimes fought, appealed to him. Winston never forgot his first ant farm, his red ants streaming like blood cells in their tunnels. He fed them sugar, bread crumbs, potato chips, and live roaches, which the ants seized and dismembered.

One day Alphonso interrupted him. "Winston, I have something to tell you. I want to tell you the truth."

The boy looked up. He thought he knew what was coming. He covered his ears.

Alphonso said, "I'm not your father. Not your real father."

Winston covered his ears. "Daddy, don't."

"Your mother was with another man."

"Daddy, Daddy," Winston said, "let's talk about something else!"

A virgin at the age of sixteen, he was introduced to sex by one of his aunts, a married woman who was bored with her husband.

Another cheating female. They slept together now and then for two years. Winston enjoyed the sex, but it also repelled him, the grappling and the smells of it.

He met Pauline Sisco in 1953. She was seventeen and he was nineteen when they married in 1955. The newlyweds moved to Brooklyn, where they lived in a taxpayer flat over a bar. Soon Pauline was sleeping with the bartender who worked downstairs. Winston bought a gun at Gimbels department store, a short-barreled carbine imported from Italy, and threatened to shoot the bartender. "We quarreled," Pauline recalled years later. Her young husband pointed the carbine at her. She snatched it away and aimed it at him.

"How does it feel to have a gun in your face?" she asked.

Winston shrugged. "Kill me. I don't care," he said.

Pauline took her finger off the trigger, a choice that would change many lives over the next decade and a half.

He filed for divorce in 1957, charging Pauline with adultery. After a New York City judge granted the divorce, Winston followed Alphonso to Queens, where the older Moseley had opened a TV and radio repair shop in Corona, the former site of the Valley of Ashes. Alphonso said TV was the future, especially color sets, and your average TV-repair bill was more than double the cost of fixing a radio.

Winston slept in Alphonso's little Corona apartment and commuted to work at Raygram in Mount Vernon. Over the years the polite, punctual machine operator earned the confidence of his boss, Abraham Zeidman. Zeidman was Jewish like Hank Greenberg; they got along. One day Zeidman said, "Moseley, you're a good worker. I'm giving you a raise to ninety a week"—a salary that worked out to more than $4,500 a year, equal to $34,000 in 2014 dollars.

On an off day, Winston struck up a conversation with a girl in a record store. Twenty-year-old Betty Grant, a nursing student, warmed to the young man with the shy smile. "He was calm and mannerly," she recalled. He knew a lot about music, down to the liner notes on the hundreds of rhythm and blues, rock 'n' roll, and classical records in his growing collection. He liked opera, too, and took Betty to several operas when they were dating. "And he never cursed, not even to say 'hell.' " They married in 1961. Betty gave birth to a son, Mark, the next year. With Winston's salary plus the eighty dollars a week she earned as a registered nurse, they could afford to put six hundred dollars down on a sixteen-thousand-dollar four-bedroom house in South Ozone Park. The mortgage was $125 a month. At home, Winston took to zoning out while he listened to his records. There were days when he barely spoke to Betty, and other days when he seemed to make up for his silences, kissing her and going on about how "perfect" she was, or hugging and kissing Mark until the baby squirmed to get away. Some evenings, Winston stopped at a bar or at Alphonso's shop on his way home from work and didn't come home until after dinner. Later he'd sit in his favorite living-room chair watching *Perry Mason* and reruns of *Rin Tin Tin* on a rabbit-ear TV Alphonso had salvaged. In the kitchen, animal-lover Winston set up an ant farm. He doted on his five German shepherds and let one of the dogs, Wolfie, sleep under Winston and Betty's bed.

His moods worried Betty, but what could she say? In many ways her Winston was a fine husband. And the Moseleys were moving up in the world. How many Negroes owned their own homes? Not one in ten. In 1963 Zeidman gave Winston another raise to a hundred dollars a week. And when Zeidman's teenage daughter needed a ride home, the boss gave the task to a man he could trust. He knew Winston Moseley would never lay a finger on the girl.

"And risk his job? Not a chance," Zeidman said later. "Winston wouldn't dare."

5

Village People

Frederick Christ Trump killed bugs cheap. The developer, whose mother's and father's surnames were Christ and Drumpf, respectively, often did his own exterminating in apartment blocks he owned, including the twenty-three-floor Coney Island apartment tower he named Trump Village. The frugal Trump went floor to floor and door to door, spraying apartments with personal-recipe pesticides. He paid a chemist to analyze name-brand products and then reformulate them with cheaper ingredients. Trump liked to say he was invested in Brooklyn and Queens, and his investments paid well enough for him to send his son Donald to the private, expensive Kew-Forest School on the town line between Kew Gardens and Forest Hills, less than a mile from the Tudor building where Kitty and Mary Ann were settling into their apartment.

In 1963 Fred Trump's weekday rounds led him past a bulldozed 240-acre expanse just north of the school, where in April Indira Gandhi, wearing a green satin sari and a hardhat, shoveled a dollop of dirt to break ground for Robert Moses's latest project, the upcoming 1964–'65 World's Fair. Gandhi's return to India later that day began with a limousine ride past the Kew-Forest School and the Genovese-Zielonko residence at 82-70 Austin Street, Kew Gardens.

Kitty and Mary Ann painted, furnished, and loved their new apartment. They worked such long hours at their respective bars that Monday, their day off, served as a one-day weekend. Sundays were rest days, "but on Mondays we acted like suburbanites," Mary Ann says. If the weather was warm, they'd open the windows and let the city's sounds in: traffic, birdsong, pedestrians' voices, barking dogs, a jackhammer, a Mister Softee truck chiming its player-piano tune. Billy Corrado, the upholsterer's son, would be throwing a baseball with Sophie and Joe Farrar's boy, Mike, on a patch of dirt behind the Tudor building while commuter trains hummed past behind them. Kitty told Mike Farrar that he reminded her of her little brothers. She often wore boys' trousers, and after she bought a new pair she'd give the old ones to Sophie, Mike's mom, so that he could have them—Kitty's hand-me-downs. Sophie scolded Mike when he scuffed them up playing dirt-patch ballgames. The boys would pretend to be Mickey Mantle and Whitey Ford, then they'd lose the ball in the fat rosebush back there and screech like schoolgirls at the scratches they got while retrieving it. Both boys figured that Kitty and Mary Ann were the best-looking roommates in Kew Gardens and maybe all of Queens. Kitty was particularly unforgettable. People remarked on how full of life she was, with a quick, wide smile and a habit of grabbing a friend's hands and doing a little dance right there on the sidewalk. Seeing Kitty walking upstairs to her apartment inspired some of Billy Corrado's first doubts about entering the priesthood.

Sometimes she and Mary Ann dropped into the Interlude Coffee House, the ground-floor café in their building where protest singer Phil Ochs led the occasional weekend sing-along. Pop polymath Al Kooper played there too. Kooper, nineteen, grew up in Hollis, around the corner from Ev's 11th Hour, the bar where Kitty worked. He played the Interlude early in the remarkable run during which he co-wrote the number-one hit "This Diamond Ring" for Gary Lewis and the Playboys, played organ on Bob Dylan's "Like a Rolling Stone," co-founded Blood, Sweat & Tears, and produced Lynyrd Skynyrd's "Sweet Home Alabama." But Kitty and Mary Ann missed most of Kooper's Interlude gigs. "We missed out because we worked weekends," Mary Ann says. "When Monday's your Saturday, you miss all the good shows."

Some Mondays they drove to Connecticut for a home-cooked Italian meal with Kitty's family. That could be awkward, with Kitty's parents asking about boyfriends. "Are you dating anyone special?" Some Mondays Kitty and Mary Ann stayed in Queens and went bowling. Mary Ann was the bowler in their circle of Kew Gardens friends, rolling games in the 120s and 130s while Kitty, laughing, might plink enough pins to break 80. "We'd get wolf whistles from beery male bowlers," Mary Ann recalls. "Sometimes worse. You get used to it." For all the world knew they were husband-hunting roommates. "We didn't act gay or butch. We weren't kissing in public. Our friends knew we were lovers, of course. I'm sure some of the neighbors suspected because we were always together, but it's not like anybody said the word 'homosexual' or 'lesbian,' even if they were thinking it. Kitty's parents knew for sure, but they were very Catholic. It's like they knew but didn't want to. It made them uncomfortable. *I* made them uncomfortable. But they tried to treat me nice, and I liked them for that."

The best Mondays, she says, "were the ones we spent in the Village." It was only half an hour from their door in the back of the Tudor building. They could spend the day in Kew Gardens, then take a twenty-minute train ride to Penn Station and go five stops downtown on the IRT subway to the center of the world.

In 1963 tourist buses ferried out-of-towners up and down the streets of Greenwich Village. Tour guides invited passengers to gawk at the folkies and beatniks, counterculture pioneers who couldn't stand each other. The beats saw the Village's nightclubs, coffeehouses, and cobblestone streets as venues for poetry readings, not singalongs. The folkies saw the beatniks as artifacts of the Eisenhower era. It was guitars battling free verse, not that either side would go in for any form of physical hostilities. They were all peaceniks, caffeine and cannabis smoothing each other out in their blood, each side convinced it had the '60s figured out.

Gerde's Folk City was a tatty nightclub at the corner of Mercer and West Fourth, next door to one of the Village's many factories, the National Tin Can Company. Folk City was known for Monday-night "hootenannies" that filled its dusty floor with foot-stomping fans. According to local legend, Pete Seeger and Woody Guthrie named their gatherings by flipping a coin to choose between the Appalachian terms *hootenanny* and *wingding*. Seeger won. As Folk City regular Joan Baez put it, "A hootenanny is to folk singing what a jam session is to jazz." Baez was twenty when she met spindly Minnesotan Bob Zimmerman, nineteen, at Folk City. This was around the time he made his professional debut there, opening for John Lee Hooker in 1961. He was Bob Dylan by then, his surname bummed from the Welsh poet who drank himself to death in '53 at the White Horse Tavern on Hudson Street, a mile away. Identities were fungible in the Village, where Leonard Schneider and Allan Konigsberg were refining standup comedy as Lenny Bruce and Woody Allen.

Dylan bunked with his teen girlfriend Suze Rotolo over an unfinished-furniture shop a couple blocks from Folk City. He introduced "Blowin' in the Wind" at a 1962 hootenanny, inspiring a pair of young folkies from Queens to ride the commuter train in from the Kew Gardens station and make their own Village debut later that year, but nobody paid much attention to Paul Simon and Art Garfunkel in those nights. Everyone was listening to Peter, Paul and Mary's number-one cover of "Blowin' in the Wind," the anthem of what one pundit called "the new national music movement."

"Kitty loved the Village. She loved the music, the people, the street life," Mary Ann says. On Bleecker Street, they passed caged chickens squawking at pedestrians. A shopkeeper sold the birds and their eggs. On Greenwich Avenue, inmates of the Women's House of Detention called through barred windows to their downtown Romeos and Juliets, and not in vain. "The jailed women's lovers, pimps, friends, and families would line up in front of the shops on Greenwich and bellow up to them at all hours," Suze Rotolo recalled. Passing the jail and its sorrowful calls and responses, Kitty and Mary Ann drew a few wolf whistles from the women behind bars, but pretended not to hear. Even in the Village, walking streets hazed with steam rising from underground vents, they wouldn't hold hands in public. As Rotolo put it, "Some things were closeted even in bohemia."

The factory-loft blocks nearby went dark after sundown, just when the lights went up at Folk City. Owner Mike Porco, lacking the mob ties that greased the local skids, had no liquor licence. He could overpay his musicians (the best got two hundred a week) because he sold coffee at the unheard-of price of $2.50 a cup. Kitty and Mary Ann used to sit at a table near the stage, drinking coffee or Cokes, holding hands under a red-checked tablecloth. The stage, a platform shoved against the back wall, was so puny that a four-person combo was always in danger of becoming a trio. Sometimes a guitarist or banjo player took a step too far and tumbled off, only to get boosted back onstage by the cheering crowd.

That Folk City stage often featured Dave Van Ronk, unofficial mayor of MacDougal Street. A broad-shouldered, bearded, glimmer-eyed Merchant Marine veteran with a worldview as jaundiced as his craggy teeth, Van Ronk had grown up in Richmond Hill, a few blocks from Kew Gardens. He was an old-school bluesman at the age of twenty-six. After turning down a chance to join Peter Yarrow and Mary Travers in a trio that would have been called Peter, Dave and Mary, he mentored Village newbies like Dylan, who came mumbling out of Hibbing, Minnesota, to surpass the rest of them. Van Ronk was put off at first by the newcomer's shifty eyes and weak, halfhearted handshake, but he liked Dylan's style. One night, he recalled, Bob Dylan spent an hour teaching everyone in the club Sioux sign language, "which I'm pretty sure he was making up as he went along." Dylan was no overnight success—more like over 1963–'64—but he was the future. Van Ronk, who never approached Dylan's star power, got a kick out of one setback his protégé encountered on the way up: In 1962, after Dylan updated Van Ronk's keening folk standard "House of the Rising Sun" on his first album, Van Ronk kept hearing that he'd swiped the song from Dylan. "People started asking me to do 'that Dylan song, the one about New Orleans.'" It pissed him off—until Eric Burdon and the Animals' cover of the tune sold more than a million copies. Now Village crowds asked to hear "that Animals song, the one about New Orleans." Dylan, disgusted, dropped it from his act.

Van Ronk was riding high in '63. "In Greenwich Village, Van Ronk was king," Dylan said. "I thought the biggest I could ever hope to get was like Van Ronk." Mary Ann and Kitty, holding hands at Folk City, feeling like natural-born Villagers, sang along with Van Ronk's

"Cocaine Blues," "Hoochie Coochie Man," "Mean Old Bedbug Blues," and his tub-thumping "Mack the Knife." They preferred Van Ronk to Dylan, Baez, Ochs, or anyone else, and preferred folk music to any other kind. Like ten or twenty thousand other Villagers, they thought the world might be changing for the better.

The Village-based folk movement spread from California to the New York island, reaching its apogee on the steps of the Lincoln Memorial in Washington, D.C., on August 28, 1963. That was the day the March on Washington preempted regular programming on all three television networks. Kitty and the regulars at Ev's 11th Hour watched on the portable TV behind the bar: Peter, Paul and Mary joining Dylan, Baez, and two hundred thousand civil-rights marchers waiting in late-summer heat to hear the Reverend Dr. Martin Luther King Jr.

Other speakers came first. John Lewis, a sharecropper's son who had overcome a stutter by preaching to chickens on his parents' farm in Alabama—and then baptizing the birds—exhorted the marchers to stop referring to themselves as "Negroes" or "colored people." They were black and ought to be proud of being black. Lewis's words would transform the nation's vocabulary, but they were forgotten for now as King delivered his seventeen-minute "I Have a Dream" speech, much of it spoken off the cuff after he lost his place in his notes. Listeners fainted in the heat as Red Cross volunteers passed out ice cubes. King hesitated. Mahalia Jackson, who had just sung the spiritual "I Been 'Buked and I Been Scorned," called out, "Tell them about the dream, Martin. Tell 'em about the dream!"

On the TV at Ev's, King raised his gaze toward the top of the screen. "Let freedom ring from every hill and molehill of Mississippi," he cried, looking forward to a day "when all of God's children, black men and white men, Jews and Gentiles, Protestants and Catholics, will be able to join hands and sing in the words of the old

Negro spiritual, 'Free at last, free at last! Thank God almighty, we are free at last!'"

Not all of Kitty's customers were looking forward to that day. Kitty enjoyed talking politics but knew that some issues were too heavy for bar chat. She smiled, kept the drinks coming, and kept her civil-rights opinions to herself.

Gay activism was another minority position. The activist Mattachine Society and the Homosexual League of New York championed gay-male rights, and the Daughters of Bilitis represented several hundred American lesbians, but with the Stonewall Riots five years in the future the vast majority of homosexuals remained in the closet. Many stepped out from time to time, particularly in New York, San Francisco, and a few other big cities. In the Village, the block between Bleecker and Third Streets got so dense with late-night hustlers that it was dubbed the Auction Block. More than a dozen Village nightclubs, all illegal, catered more or less exclusively to gay people. Under New York law, serving a single drink to a homosexual ("sexual deviate" in the statute) made a club or restaurant a "disorderly house" by definition, subject to a fine or the loss of the club's liquor license. Two women dancing together, two men kissing, or anyone cross-dressing constituted disorderly conduct. The law was a boon to organized crime, which ran the profitable underground gay clubs, and to the policemen who collected payoffs to let them stay in business. In the early '60s the Village was home to gay-male bars including the Gold Bug, lesbian bars like the Swing Rendezvous and Bonnie and Clyde's, and some that swung both ways. At the Ace of Clubs, a lesbian hangout that was one of Mary Ann's favorites, the music was soft enough to permit conversation. The Bagatelle was more hardcore and, to Kitty, more thrilling. According to poet Audre Lorde, the smoky Bagatelle reeked of "beer and lots of good-looking young women." Femmes at "the Bag" wore slinky dresses and slow-danced "garrison belt to pubis and rump to rump" with butch partners who flattened their breasts with ACE bandages and wore suits, ties, and fedoras.

At a time when no shopkeeper could openly sell sex toys, even in the Village, downtowners fashioned dildos from crutch cushions, the green rubber pads that fit the tops of crutches to protect users' armpits. Those makeshift dildos made a notable bulge in the baggiest trousers. Sometimes topped with a condom to look more like a penis, they were called green hornets. At the Bagatelle, one of the few spots where Kitty felt free to touch her partner and dance like a sexual being, she would laugh when a green hornet slipped down someone's pant leg and got kicked around the dance floor in an impromptu game of soccer.

"If the lights flashed red, it was a signal," Mary Ann says. "It meant stop dancing, the police are coming. Somebody always tipped off the manager." The cops would barge in to find a roomful of women standing around talking. Or not talking—just watching New York's Finest carry out their crooked errand. It was usually two or three angry-looking officers, sticking close together as if the room might be infectious. After making sure there were no sex acts in progress, they proceeded to the manager's office. The women waited out the interruption, lighting cigarettes, whispering, lining up for the ladies' room, or finding a place to sit while the harsh houselights revealed bubble-gum blots on the floor, water stains on the ceiling, and wrinkles on the faces and hands of weary dancers who had looked younger before the lights came up.

A certain stripe of vice cop enjoyed raiding lesbian clubs. Rather than pocket his payoff and leave, this kind liked to have a little fun with the customers. He would wave his badge or billy club, saying he was there to enforce city ordinances banning public lewdness, including cross-dressing. He might check the patrons' identification.

(One customer was so afraid to be outed that she ate her driver's license.) Or he might pick someone out for a strip search. Women were required by law to wear a certain amount of women's clothes—one ordinance called for at least three articles of gender-appropriate clothing. There were cops who liked to shove a hand down a cross-dresser's pants and say, "So you think you're a man? Let's see what you've got down there." Any green hornets that turned up could be confiscated as evidence.

Mary Ann dreaded vice raids. She could hardly bear the thought of some leering cop's looking down Kitty's slacks to prove she wasn't wearing B.V.D.s. "We hated the cops," she says, "but they didn't scare us as much as the queer-hunters." Gangs of young men were known to roam the Village late at night, looking for trouble. "Some of them were soldiers, but mostly they were just Italian guys looking for gay people to beat up. We had a friend, Bunny, who dressed in drag. They whipped Bunny with bike chains." Unlike Mitch, the six-foot bartender who got beaten to death, Bunny survived. "Even in the Village, or especially in the Village, you couldn't be gay and feel safe." As much as Kitty and Mary Ann relished their Monday-night adventures in Manhattan, they felt safer when they stepped off the train at the Kew Gardens station, a hundred yards from their door.

The top record of 1963 was a comedy album. *The First Family* featured the Boston-bred Greenwich Village comic Vaughn Meader's near-perfect impression of President Kennedy. "We shall move ahead with great vig-ah," Meader intoned on the fastest-selling album ever, a surprise blockbuster that led the president to open a press conference by quipping, "Vaughn Meader was busy tonight, so I came myself." Kennedy adopted another hit record, the soundtrack of the Broadway smash *Camelot*, as a theme of his administration, imitating Richard Burton ("Don't let it be forgot . . .") while digging his own spadeful of dirt at the site of the New York World's Fair.

Then it was Friday afternoon, November 22. "We were both at work," Mary Ann recalls. "They broke in on TV and said the president had been shot." Seventy minutes after the shooting, Dallas police arrested ex-Marine Lee Harvey Oswald. Town meetings, PTA meetings, football and basketball games were canceled from coast to coast. Only later would that Friday be seen as a dividing line between a more innocent time and a darker era to come. Mary Ann recalls feeling a chill. "Maybe it was that day plus the missile crisis the year before, but just getting up in the morning, going to work, felt different, like something bad could happen today."

Lenny Bruce agreed that things were different. On the night after Kennedy was shot, Bruce made his scheduled appearance in Greenwich Village. Ready to offend as usual, he stepped into the spotlight, shook his head sadly and addressed the unavoidable issue. "Man," he said, "Vaughn Meader is fucked."

A month later, Mary Ann stood at her easel in the book-strewn living room she and Kitty shared, painting snow on the roof of a country church. She had to wait for the canvas to stop shivering whenever a train passed outside. "That was our one Christmas together," she says. "I did some painting, then we drove up to Connecticut to see her family." The lovers stuck a few presents in Kitty's 1963 Fiat and took the Hutchinson River Parkway past the brown brick tenements of the Bronx to woodsy Merritt Parkway, an hour's drive through light snow to New Canaan, Kitty behind the wheel. Pulling into the driveway of her parents' house on Riverbank Court, a postcard ranch house with Christmas lights framing the windows, Kitty led the way to the porch.

Her parents were in their fifties by then. Vinny was going gray, but his wife wouldn't have to, thanks to Miss Clairol, the hair-color treatment with the TV commercials asking, "Does she . . . or doesn't she? Only her hairdresser knows for sure."

"The girls are here!" Hugging her daughter, Rachel showed the two of them to the living room, where Kitty's four siblings greeted their big sister like a celebrity. Vincent, twenty-five, might try to play it cool, but seventeen-year-old Susan, fifteen-year-old Bill, and twelve-year-old Frank crowded around her, pointing out gifts under the Christmas tree, asking Kitty to guess what they'd gotten her. "A real nice family Christmas," Mary Ann calls it.

Judy Garland, one of the Kennedys' Hollywood friends, had tried to cancel her CBS Christmas special that year. Who wanted to sing "Jingle Bells" in such a dark time? The network appealed to her patriotism, saying the country needed good cheer now more than ever, and there she was on the Genoveses' living room TV, starring in a *Judy Garland Christmas Special* brought to you by Pall Mall cigarettes ("You can light either end. Outstanding . . . *and* they are mild") and Contac, "the capsule with the tiny time pills." Garland belted carols with teenage daughter Liza and closed the show with a mournful "Over the Rainbow."

Somebody put a record on the hi-fi. Andy Williams's *Christmas Album* featured the crooner's top-forty cover of "White Christmas" and a newly minted standard, "It's the Most Wonderful Time of the Year," with its amusing lines about "the hap-happiest season of all" and "gay happy meetings when friends come to call." A pair of bohemian lesbians exchanging private glances over cookies and eggnog, Kitty and Mary Ann felt hap-happy to be anywhere "as long as we were together," Mary Ann says. She remembers the glances Kitty's parents exchanged. Devout Catholics who saw gay sex as sinful, Vinny and Rachel Genovese surely wished their daughter had never met Mary Ann, the siren they blamed for leading her into temptation. They didn't want to imagine Kitty's life with another woman any more than Mary Ann wanted to see a vice cop frisk their daughter. Vinny used to drive to Kew Gardens now and then to take Kitty to lunch, but he refused to set foot in their apartment. Their lesbian apartment. He waited in his car until Kitty came downstairs. "I'm sure they thought we were going to hell, or at least I was," Mary Ann says. She and Kitty slept separately in Kitty's parents' house.

On Christmas morning they exchanged presents. Kitty gave Mary Ann a black leather billfold, and Mary Ann gave Kitty a matching brown billfold. The rest of the Genoveses went to Christmas Mass while Kitty and Mary Ann drove back to the city.

6

She Loves You

Time magazine opened 1964 by putting Martin Luther King Jr. on its cover. On January 6, *Time*'s Man of the Year sat in the gallery at the Supreme Court in Washington, D.C., hearing arguments in *New York Times Co. v. Sullivan*, a press-freedom case that threatened to land him in prison. That evening King returned to his room in Washington's Willard Hotel, which the FBI had bugged. J. Edgar Hoover's agents listened in as King and a couple of friends caroused with women who were not their wives. "This will destroy the burrhead," said a gleeful Hoover, who informed President Lyndon Johnson that *Time*'s saintly Man of the Year was "a tomcat with obsessive degenerate sexual urges." This from a G-man who was rumored to be a closeted cross-dresser. Everyone seemed to be hiding something.

Nineteen sixty-four would be a new year of upheaval. "On January 1, the dourest observer of the passing scene could not foresee a country in which students would rise up against their elders, city dwellers would set fire to their neighborhoods, and women would begin to wonder whether the male sex was their oppressor," wrote the *Chicago Tribune*'s Jon Margolis. With Kitty working double shifts, Mary Ann spent some of her afternoons alone in their apartment. She put aside her painting of a snow-covered church and started a new canvas, a portrait of Kitty on a park bench, the wind in her hair.

Kitty didn't complain about her long hours behind the bar at Ev's. Her outgoing personality made her a natural for the job. "She had the gift of gab," Mary Ann says. And there was so much to talk about. For one thing, President Johnson was pushing hard for passage of Kennedy's civil-rights program. Kitty didn't mind saying she thought LBJ was doing a good job. For another thing, the U.S. Surgeon General announced for the first time that cigarettes could kill you—unwelcome news to Kitty, Mary Ann, and eighty million other American smokers. People were also talking about the wildly popular new Volkswagen Beetle (Kitty swore by her still-smaller Fiat), those funny Clampetts on TV's top-rated *Beverly Hillbillies*, and a pair of film comedies that exemplified changing times, the kitschy *It's a Mad Mad Mad Mad World* and *Dr. Strangelove*, Stanley Kubrick's ink-black rejoinder to the Cuban Missile Crisis. On the radio, Bobby Vinton's sappy "There! I've Said It Again" held the number-one spot and one other distinction: it was the last number-one tune before the Beatles took over the charts.

The year before, New York music producer Sid Bernstein, a forty-five-year-old scrabbler hoping to widen his horizons, took a journalism course from Max Lerner at the New School. Reading newspapers from England, Bernstein kept spotting the name of a new band from Liverpool. "Every week the font of the stories about them got bigger," he recalled. Without hearing a note of their music he arranged to fly the Beatles to New York. Bernstein booked Carnegie Hall for three thousand dollars—most of his savings—after convincing the hall's legendary booking manager, Ioana Satescu, that the Beatles were worthy. "I said, 'Mrs. Satescu, they're an incredible group!' She thought I meant a chamber group, a string quartet." On February 7, 1964, Pan Am Flight 101 carried John Lennon, Paul McCartney, George Harrison, and Ringo Starr from London to Queens. Five thousand screaming fans and 110 police officers met their flight at the newly named John F. Kennedy Airport. Kitty and her customers followed the moptops' progress on the bar TV at Ev's. That Sunday night, with almost half of America tuning in to see them on *The Ed Sullivan Show*, Sullivan announced that the boys had just received a good-luck telegram from none other than Elvis Presley. Harrison cracked, "Elvis who?" The Beatles opened their five-song set with "All My Loving" and closed with "I Want to Hold Your Hand," and for the second time in three months the world changed forever. After the Sullivan show they twisted the night away at the Peppermint Lounge. On February 24, *Newsweek*, the first American magazine to put the Beatles on its cover, ran a slam: "Visually they are a nightmare . . . musically a near-disaster. Their lyrics (punctuated by nutty shouts of yeah yeah yeah) are a catastrophe." By then the band had played Carnegie Hall, where booker Satescu shot Sid Bernstein a dark look and told him, "Never come back again."

Kitty and Mary Ann liked the Beatles. They might not be up there with Van Ronk, but they were as cute as their two-minute tunes. And around the end of February, with "I Want to Hold Your Hand" and "She Loves You" numbers one and two on the charts, Kitty announced that she wanted to do more dancing. "We don't dance as much as we used to. We could learn to salsa," she said. Mary

Ann, who was happy enough staying home, painting her lover's picture or reading a book, said all right to more dancing. "I wanted her to be happy." She thought the two of them were just different enough to last as a couple. "I was always more 'out' than Kitty was, with her Catholic background and Catholic family, but she was getting happier. She was more vibrant than ever in those days, becoming the person she really wanted to be."

They spent an occasional afternoon across the hall in the Farrars' apartment, sipping coffee at Sophie's kitchen table. Petite strawberry-blonde Sophie, who stood four foot eleven, was one of the few people who literally looked up to five-foot-one Kitty. Neighbor Billy Corrado recalls Sophie as "a spunky lady. Her husband Joe worked for the railroad. He was a big guy, and she only went up to his shoulders." A devoutly Catholic fish-on-Fridays mother of two, Sophie reminded Kitty of her own mother. Maybe that was why Kitty shared a secret with her. Once, when it was just the two of them talking over coffee, she told Sophie about her 1959 church wedding to an Army man in Connecticut. The match had delighted Kitty's parents, but it didn't last. Kitty's marriage was annulled, apparently unconsummated, only two months after the wedding. In the eyes of the church it never happened.

This is what Kitty confided to Sophie. Kitty always identified herself as a lesbian. She wasn't ashamed to be who she was. She was happy, she said, but still there were times when she envied Sophie's "normal" life. "Your family and this place," she said, looking around the Farrars' apartment strewn with toys. "I think I'd like something like this." Not because she didn't love Mary Ann; in fact, speaking of envy, she couldn't help envying Mary Ann's clear idea of her own sexuality. Still there was something she and Mary Ann could never have. "Children," she told Sophie. "I'd like to have children." The trouble was that intercourse with a man was physically painful for her. That was why her marriage had failed. A doctor had told her that an operation could help. It was a simple procedure. She was young; she might still have children. The thought of surgery worried Kitty, but she was thinking about it. "Maybe I could be a mom like you," she said.

Sophie and her family kept Kitty's words to themselves for fifty years.

Mary Ann, the practical partner, wanted them to keep to a household budget. Kitty could have done it; she kept the books at the bar. At home, however, her idea of planning for the future was picturing the *ristorante* she hoped to open someday, a romantic place with white tablecloths, Chianti bottles in wicker baskets, and family recipes on the menu. One day she said, "I want to go to Italy."

Mary Ann said, "Why?"

"To *see* it."

"How much would it cost?"

"Who cares?"

When they quarreled, their friend Angelo Lanzone recalls, "it was usually about money. Usually—like always." Lanzone worked at the airport, driving a forklift for Pan Am, and gave his friends tips on horse races at the local track. He'd stop by Ev's when Kitty was on duty. "She was real generous to people in the bar, lending them five or ten or twenty dollars," he says. Twenty dollars was about half what Kitty earned in a typical shift. "She didn't care. She liked everybody. She never got much of her money back, and Mary Ann was always telling her to cut it out." Lanzone used to meet the two of them for dinner at the Hofbrau, a venerable German restaurant once favored by Mae West, Babe Ruth, and songsmith Chancellor Olcott, who wrote "When Irish Eyes Are Smiling" there in 1912. "I remember one day, we sit down and right away the girls start going on about money. Pretty soon Kitty gets up and leaves in a huff. Mary Ann and I finish eating, and when I go to pay the bill, the manager says we had three dinners. I said, 'No, two.' Three, he says. I flat refuse to pay for three, and he kicks us out. 'And stay out!' he says. Those girls squabbling about money got me banned from the Hofbrau!"

Mike Farrar, Sophie and Joe's twelve-year-old son, recalls seeing Kitty and Mary Ann "yelling and fighting" on the landing outside their apartment, "and they knocked each other right down the stairs." But they always made up. After walking out of the Hofbrau, Kitty apologized with a peace offering. She bought a black poodle from Karl Ross, a neighbor in the Tudor building who ran a dog-grooming shop, and gave the dog to Mary Ann.

"Kitty told me she was sorry," Mary Ann recalls, "and she gave me that poodle—Andrew, we called him—and we loved him. He was part of our little family. Having a dog in the apartment made it more like a real home."

She remembers their neighbor Ross, the dog groomer, as "a very nervous, frightened person." He was slim, balding, thirty-one years old. "We knew he was gay, but he tried to hide it." Ross lived two doors down from Kitty and Mary Ann. "He had a shop in the neighborhood, but he was so shy it was all he could do to leave his apartment and go there." What Ross liked to do was drink, and once he learned that there were fellow bohemians in the building he began turning up at their door, sometimes with a bottle. If nobody answered his knock he might let himself in, the way Sophie did when she answered the phone. Ross was a welcome guest, the perfect dog sitter for Andrew the poodle. If Kitty happened to be home, she would pour Ross a drink and chat with him about LBJ, civil rights, dogs, and neighborhood news as the radio mumbled on the windowsill. Never much of a drinker, Kitty would water down a vodka for herself and sip it for an hour while Ross nursed the bottle. Or she'd pour herself a rum-and-Coke that was 95 percent Coke. Later, when she and Mary Ann were alone discussing the day, they would talk about poor Karl Ross, scared of his shadow, trying to drink his fears away. They thought of Ross as a stray they were sheltering.

7

Ozone Park

During their courtship in 1960 and early '61, Winston Moseley took Betty to parties. Sometimes she talked him into dancing. Now and then he would play poker—five-card stud—with other young men or shoot dice with them, talking baseball. "We didn't have any friends, though," Betty recalled, and after their wedding, they stayed home every night. Her husband prized his quiet time. He'd sit on the couch or at the kitchen table, his delicate features settling into a blank expression. When she asked what he was doing, he said, "Thinking. Just thinking."

He heard Malcolm X talking on the radio about white devils and race war. He heard Martin Luther King preaching about turning the other cheek. Winston could see things both ways. He was peaceful, even timid, but with a temper. He remembered a night when he came upon Alphonso and a teenager fighting. The boy had a knife; he was cutting Alphonso's face. Winston would usually cross the street to avoid a mean-looking man, but seeing this kid attack Alphonso set off a tripwire in him. He grabbed a Pepsi bottle and smashed the kid's face. The boy lost an eye. Winston's attack might have landed him in jail had the teenager been white, but the participants were all black, and a grand jury ruled that no crime had occurred. His courage got him a hug from the man he still called Daddy, but before long Fannie was back in the picture, fighting with Alphonso over family matters. Alphonso couldn't believe that Winston let his mother stay overnight in his house. A crazy house, Alphonso called it. Wife, kids, dogs, ants, and a witch! How could Winston let Fannie set foot in his home? Hadn't she cheated on Alphonso and run out on both of them?

Winston shrugged.

He enjoyed his own company and that of his dogs. He could spend an hour grooming the dogs, then turn to his own hair and nails. A neat freak who sometimes washed his hands, dried them, and then washed them again, he took his time clipping and filing the nails on his fingers and toes, trimming his threadlike goatee, combing his hair. Keeping himself sharp. He said a man needed to look sharp, a Negro especially.

He was a solid provider. Just as important to his mother, Winston was a good citizen. "He was kind and gentle," said Fannie, who was now the picture of health two decades after using a trip to the hospital as an excuse to escape her family. Her son forgave her. To his wife's chagrin, Winston even invited Fannie to move into the house in South Ozone Park—not just overnight, but for good.

Winston and Betty's year-old son, Mark, was learning to walk that winter. They also took in another child, Kerry, whose fourteen-year-old mother was a cousin of Winston's. They planned to adopt the child—a good deed and a great favor for the baby and the Moseleys' extended family. As Winston approached his thirtieth birthday he was by all appearances a settled, successful young man, a solid citizen. He still doted on his ants and the five purebred German shepherds that shared the house. His favorite dog was Wolfie, the watchdog that slept under Winston and Betty's bed. Wolfie had bitten visitors, including Alphonso, whose TV repair shop in Corona was one of Winston's hangouts. Alphonso could have made a stink about the dog bite, but he let it go, perhaps because Winston kept showing up with TVs and radios for Alphonse to sell, no questions asked.

Winston offered to do his daddy another favor. Once, when Alphonso began following Fannie around the neighborhood in his car, waving a pistol and threatening to "put a bullet in the bitch," Winston told him to stop acting crazy. He didn't want Alphonso getting in trouble with the police.

"Give me the gun, Daddy. Let me do it," he said. "I'll shoot Mommy for you."

Alphonso handed over the gun. He was never sure if Winston intended to use it or if he was only trying to save Alphonso from himself. Winston had at least one gun of his own, so maybe he really was trying to keep Alphonso out of prison. Winston had plenty of chances to shoot his mother now that Fannie, the skilled survivor, was sitting with her feet up in Winston's drafty house near the airport, but he never so much as waved the pistol at her.

The Moseleys paid their taxes, kept their grass trimmed, and went on the same outings to Rockaway Beach and Coney Island that other families took. Winston polished the woodwork inside his house until it gleamed. He built a fence around the yard so that the neighborhood kids wouldn't bother his dogs and vice versa. Still Betty fretted about her husband.

Winston had always been shy. He couldn't bring himself to undress in front of his wife. Instead he'd shut off the lights or retreat to the bathroom to take off his clothes. Over the winter of 1963–'64 his bodily discomfort seemed to grow. He and Betty hardly ever had sex. She told herself it was understandable, with him working days at Raygram and her working nights at Elmhurst Hospital. During the week they would tape a note to their front door to deter visitors: *WORKING NIGHTS. MUST SLEEP DURING THE DAY. PLEASE DO NOT DISTURB UNNECESSARILY.* By the weekend, when they finally had a few hours to themselves, they were worn out. They had enjoyed what Betty considered a normal sex life early in their marriage, but now her husband was usually impotent. He would arouse himself by performing oral sex on her, which she tolerated, hoping for more. As a registered nurse, twenty-four-year-old Betty considered herself fairly enlightened about sex, but she worried. As she testified later before a judge and jury, their marital relations "went from what you'd call normal to what they describe as cunnilingus."

After one of their infrequent sexual encounters, Betty woke before dawn to find her husband's side of the bed empty. The next morning he said he'd gone for a drive. On other nights he knocked around the house late at night, fiddling with appliances. Sometimes an extra toaster or TV set appeared on the kitchen counter. "For Daddy," he said, as if that explained it.

His grooming slipped. Fussy, deliberate Winston, who never had a hair out of place, began skipping showers. He seemed never to sleep.

"Do you want to see a doctor?" Betty asked.

"Why?" he asked. "There's lots of people sicker than me."

She wasn't the only one to notice a change in him. Alphonso asked if something was wrong. "No, nothing, Daddy."

On weekday mornings he slept until seven, when Betty phoned

from the hospital to wake him. After his wakeup call, Winston shaved and showered. He fed the dogs. If there was fresh ground beef in the refrigerator, he'd give Wolfie a bite as a treat. On cold mornings he'd go out around 8:20 to start his car, a white 1960 Corvair tinged gray with grime and street salt after four New York winters. He had taken out a loan to buy the car and faithfully kept up on his payments of forty-five dollars a month. Like millions of upwardly mobile Americans, he and Betty were a two-car couple. He'd start the Corvair, switch on the heater, and go back inside to wait for Betty to get home from the hospital, driving the '62 Ford Fairlane he had bought her. He'd kiss her good morning and set off for work.

Winston's commute took him past construction crews, electricians, and landscapers hurrying to prepare the grounds and exhibition halls of the World's Fair, scheduled to open in April. Master planner Robert Moses had been working overtime himself, completing Lincoln Center after his crews razed the Hell's Kitchen setting of *West Side Story* to make room for it. The seventy-five-year-old Moses was also finishing the $325 million Verrazano-Narrows Bridge connecting Brooklyn and Staten Island, with its seven-hundred-foot towers and ten-thousand-ton cables, at the time the world's longest suspension bridge. But the fair was his pet project. More than the greatest show on earth, Moses wanted it to be the greatest in history. A team of metalworking Mohawks imported from Quebec was putting final touches on the fair's centerpiece, a silver model of the globe complete with elliptical steel ribbons representing astronauts' orbits. Fifty years later, the twelve-story, 350-ton Unisphere would still be the largest model of the planet ever built. Moses described it as "a huge stainless-steel globe ringed with satellites to emphasize our loneliness in space." *Esquire* described it as "incredibly corny." But then Moses was as proudly square as *Camelot*. Eighteen months after Kennedy called for America to put a man on the moon "before this decade is out," Moses's fair would employ Broadway tunes, Disney spectacle, and Cold War science to bring a space-age future to the site of the old Corona dump. NASA wouldn't reach the moon for another five years, but Moses's fair already boasted a prototype of the Apollo program's lunar module as well as the world's first picture-phone; a computer-telephone link called a modem; a display showing future forests being chopped down by laser beams; and deep-sea homes with two-submarine garages. The world was improving thanks to science, industry, and American know-how.

The fair's Tent of Tomorrow held a kitchen of the future with a nuclear oven (microwaves were for the radio telescopes in NASA's exhibit) and a dishwasher that crushed dirty plastic plates into pellets, which were re-formed into clean new dishes. The Hall of Presidents, whose design Kennedy had approved two days before his assassination, featured a lock of Andrew Jackson's hair as well as Lincoln's stovepipe hat and Gettysburg Address, Theodore Roosevelt's Rough Rider uniform, Truman's THE BUCK STOPS HERE desk sign, and JFK's rocking chair. In the Vatican Pavilion stood Michelangelo's *Pietà*, making its first road trip since its unveiling in 1499. Exhibitors hired Broadway set designer Jo Mielziner, who had staged *Annie Get Your Gun*, to add pizzazz to the three-thousand-pound sculpture depicting Jesus dead in his mother's arms. Mielziner added a Gregorian-chant soundtrack and hundreds of blue candles sparkling behind bulletproof glass.

At Sinclair Oil's Dinoland, nine fiberglass saurians still lacked a coat of paint as opening day loomed. The fair's guidebook blamed the dinosaurs' extinction not on an asteroid impact, unimagined at the time, but on our kind: "Ancient mammals learned to eat their enormous eggs." But not even a life-size *Tyrannosaurus rex* could overshadow the fair's most sensational attraction: Walt Disney's "audio-animatronic" Lincoln, the world's most lifelike robot. Seeing and hearing Honest Abe in the rubberized flesh, with forty-eight body movements, seventeen pre-programmed head movements, and a face made from Lincoln's death mask, would move some fairgoers to tears.

For a baseball fan like Winston Moseley the main attraction of Moses's construction project may have been the giant cement bowl rising beside the fairgrounds. When it opened in April, Shea Stadium, the state-of-the-art home of the New York Metropolitans, would feature twenty-five escalators instead of the traditional concrete ramps, plus blue and orange neon piping and an eight-story video scoreboard. Manager Casey Stengel's Mets had improved from a historically awful 40–120 record in their inaugural season of 1962 ("Can't anybody here play this game?" Stengel asked) to 51–111 the following year. "We are a much-improved ballclub," baseball's Old Perfessor announced. "Now we can lose in extra innings."

Mets pitchers and catchers were loosening up at their spring-training fields in St. Petersburg, Florida, as Moseley motored past their new stadium on his way to work. Fifteen to twenty minutes later he pulled into Raygram's blacktop parking lot in Mount Vernon. Aside from a coffee break and a half hour for lunch, he would spend the next nine hours running machines that punched holes in computer cards. There was a lunchroom down the hall, but Moseley preferred his own company. He brought lunch from home and ate it at his desk.

The computer cards he produced were first-generation software: stiff paper rectangles measuring seven and three-eighths inches by three and a quarter, rounded at the corners, emblazoned with the motto *Methods That Keynote the Future of Business.* The holes he punched in them encoded information that later computers would process in a fraction of the time by tracking electrons on circuit boards, rendering hole-punchers like Moseley obsolete. The Remington Rand computers that used Raygram's cards tallied business accounts faster than ever before, but they were primitive compared to the machines NASA was developing at the same time. The space program's massive mainframes would soon calculate trajectories precisely enough to guide a two-ton Apollo capsule a quarter of a million miles from the earth to meet the moon in its path around the planet, then slingshot the capsule into lunar orbit, and finally bring it home safely—a feat that seems all the more miraculous considering that the computers employed in NASA's moon missions had about half the computing power of a 2014 smartphone.

Moseley used his Remington Rand machine to program Raygram's inventory. It was drudgework, but he was good at it. A smart man like him could devote a small part of his mind to his work while the rest churned with private thoughts.

8

The 11th Hour

Kitty was dressing for work. It was March 12. Tomorrow it would be a year to the day since she met Mary Ann at the Swing, a day to dance and have a drink. But today was just another Thursday, another double shift at the bar.

It was cold out. The cold had frosted the bedroom window overlooking the sidewalk. She rolled nylon stockings up legs she considered a little too short. So maybe her legs weren't her best feature, who's perfect? Kitty was the type of person who believes that you do the best you can with what you've got. Not one to put on airs or brood or mope, she accentuated the positive. Her style was spruce, a term that meant fresh, not fancy but a step up from what you'd see in the usual crowd around the Kew Gardens train station.

Nylons for starters. Then a slenderizing girdle with garters. After she clipped her stockings to the girdle, she added a black half-slip with lace trim, then a lightly padded bra. Most people who met her remembered her dark hair and pretty face, but she was sensitive about her small bust. The bra gave her a little more confidence. Next she buttoned up a gray flannel skirt. No boys' pants for work; she tried to look nice on the job. She picked a turquoise blouse from the closet—a touch of color—and topped her ensemble with a suede jacket. Last came a gold Speidel bracelet inscribed *KITTY*.

Wearing black leather pumps comfortable enough for twelve-plus hours on her feet, Kitty walked by the Interlude Coffee House in chilly fog. Turning right, she passed the drugstore, where a new issue of *Vogue* held the magazine's first-ever feature on miniskirts. Her Fiat waited steps away, a bright red two-seater that looked like a cherry gumdrop on wheels. She unlocked the driver's door. Many of the cars on the block were left unlocked. Kitty locked hers not because there was much crime on her block but because the Fiat was her proudest possession. Its fifteen-horsepower engine started grudgingly, coughing white exhaust. She nosed it into traffic. She could always count on the heater to kick in just as she reached her destination. She wove through traffic, slipping between Fairlanes and T-Birds, Dodge Darts, VW Beetles, and wide-grilled Catalinas. Kitty liked to drive fast. She zipped through Jamaica Hills to 193rd Street in Hollis, Queens, and tucked into a parking space on Jamaica Avenue.

A hole-in-the-wall tavern with a deli to the left, cheap apartments to the right, and a starved-looking tulip tree planted in the sidewalk out front, Ev's 11th Hour was the sort of place you could miss if you drove by too fast. Its plain façade featured a rectangular window that reminded World War II veterans of a German pillbox. But Ev's was cozy enough inside, a shot-and-a-beer kind of bar with knotty pine–paneled walls, the kind of bar stools that need a matchbook under one leg to stay level, and a few booths along the back wall by the jukebox. "Just a neighborhood joint," recalls bartender Victor Horan, who lived around the corner. "We had Piels and Rheingold on tap, ballgames on the bar TV."

Kitty usually took the day shift, 9:00 a.m. till 6:00 p.m., when Horan came in. She also managed the place for owner Evelyn Randolph, who lived in New Jersey. "Kitty was in charge, and she was good at it," Horan recalls. "She was a good boss, very low key. She had a nice smile. The customers liked her. You never heard anybody say a bad word about Kitty." Horan says nobody could tell a drinker he'd had enough as gently and firmly as she could—and still get a good tip from the guy. She also did the bookkeeping, paid Horan and their suppliers, deposited cash in the owner's bank account, paid the plumber when the toilet backed up, or the locksmith or electrician when they needed one, and paid herself, apparently without dipping into the till as so many bartenders and managers did. "Kitty wouldn't do that. She did things right," Horan says.

Customers liked her smile and friendly, topical patter as well as the small loans she made out of the brown billfold Mary Ann had given her for Christmas. Kitty saw the loans as a kindness as well as a sort of recycling, since the regulars spent their money on drinks and tips when they weren't betting on horses or playing the numbers.

Numbers games were illegal but popular in all five boroughs. Sometimes called Italian lotteries, a tip of the fedora to their sixteenth-century origins in Italy and modern Mafia backing, the rackets allowed bettors to risk their dimes and dollars on any number between 1 and 1,000. Bartenders sometimes booked the bets. More often, numbers runners performed the same service, collecting dollars and jotting bettors' three-digit choices in notebooks or on betting slips. They would deliver the day's wagers and betting slips to the local numbers bank, which might be the back room of a pool hall or social club.

There, in the simplest version of the racket, low-level mobsters drew lots or spun a wheel to select the day's winning number. With rare exceptions they ran an honest game. They could afford to, because the racket generated far better profits than the 5 to 10 percent rake that financed the casinos of Las Vegas and Atlantic City. Of course everything is relative. Even the greediest numbers racket paid out about six hundred dollars for every thousand wagered, for a rake of 40 percent. High, but still lower than that of the legal lotteries that would put them out of business. The typical rake for today's state-run scratch-offs, Lottos, and Powerball games is 50 percent. As one wiseguy put it, "A lottery is a tax on people who don't understand mathematics."

By the 1960s the games had long since grown too profitable to be decided by spinning a wheel in a pool hall, a system that invited suspicions that the fix might be in. To inspire confidence among players, the mobsters needed a random-number generator. They found it in the daily reports of the New York Stock Exchange. At the close of each day's trading, the NYSE reported the number of shares traded. The three middle digits of its daily report became that day's winning number. If 25,217,880 shares had changed hands, anyone who had put a dollar on 217 was a winner. A runner delivered a payoff of about six hundred dollars cash. There were other ways to generate a winning number—some games used the final three digits of the published daily balance of the U.S. Treasury, or three digits from the handle at a race track, digits that kept widows, bus drivers, barbers, dog groomers, and a few stockbrokers listening to financial reports or race results on the radio to find out if this was their lucky day.

Booking numbers was only one of a bartender's sidelines. It was a horse racing bet that got Kitty arrested.

She liked to bet a few dollars on the harness races at Roosevelt Raceway, a half-mile track in Westbury, New York, half an hour east on Long Island. Angelo Lanzone had a friend in the paddock there, a man who gave him an occasional tip on a fixed race. Lanzone would tell Kitty, warning her to keep it to herself, but she promptly spread the word to Mary Ann and the regulars at the bar. "That's no way to treat a sure thing, but she was just being nice," Lanzone says.

Back in 1961, two years before she met Mary Ann, Kitty had been living with a girlfriend named Dolores "Dee" Guarnieri. Dee worked at a tavern called the Emerald Bar & Grill in Rosedale, Queens. Kitty was tending bar at the Queens Café nearby. One day an undercover policeman, Walter Newman, asked Guarnieri to place a bet for him. The customer she knew as "Wally" said he wanted to put four dollars on a Daily Double entry, Rash Action and Fleet John, plus five on another horse. Rash Action was the number-two horse, Fleet John the number-four horse. Guarnieri took his nine dollars—as a favor, she said—and phoned Kitty at the Queens Café.

"Rash Action and Fleet John, two and four reverse," Dee said, meaning a two-four Daily Double and a four-two, "plus five on Madame Bob to win." Kitty wrote it down.

Two hours later, Patrolman Newman arrested Kitty. According to newly discovered courtroom transcripts, Newman later swore that he "identified [him]self to Genovese and placed her under arrest." Kitty "stated she has only been doing this for a month," Newman reported, "and that she gets five percent of the action handled." She was probably joking about her cut of the action. Sounding sarcastic, she told the patrolman, "Right! I take in thousands a day and I get five percent." She knew that what she had done was illegal, but didn't necessarily think it was wrong.

On September 5, 1961, Kitty reported to City Magistrates Court, also known as Gamblers' Court. She was charged with operating an illegal gambling enterprise, a misdemeanor. During her brief trial, Patrolman Newman and his partner, Robert Monroe, described staking out the Emerald Bar & Grill and the Queens Café two weeks earlier, eavesdropping on the bartenders. At one point Monroe pretended to go to the men's room, then circled back to pick up a Piels coaster Dee Guarnieri had dropped after using it to write down the bet. Their sting operation required days of two officers' time to nab two young women over a nine-dollar wager. The whole thing seemed silly, but by the morning of her court date Kitty was taking it seriously. She had no criminal record.

On the witness stand, she gave her name and occupation. "I'm a barmaid." Or had been, she said, until she got fired from her job at the café after getting arrested. She admitted placing an occasional bet with a bookie named Louis—a couple dollars on the harness races at Aqueduct. "I like the trotters. If this fellow comes in and I happen to want to bet a trotter, that's my bet. Two dollars."

Defense attorney Sidney Sparrow asked Kitty to describe her arrest.

"Dolores called me up," she said, "and asked me if I could put a bet in. I said, 'If he comes around. If he doesn't, I won't.' Around two o'clock three men were sitting at the bar, this officer Newman and two other fellows, drinking and laughing. All of a sudden the red-headed fellow says, 'Come here, Kitty.' He said, 'I'm a police officer. We know all about you.' I said, 'About what?' He said, 'You have been taking bets for a long time.' He kept insisting I was in with these big racketeers, taking bets for them. I didn't know what he was talking about until he mentioned Dolores. I told him, 'She called me about a bet, but I didn't do anything about it.' They didn't believe anything I said. He said I was a member of a big organization."

Officer Newman surely knew that the Genovese crime family ran the numbers and other rackets in much of the city. Kitty had an Uncle Vito who shared the Mafia don's name—a source of confusion to those who would follow her story later. Her uncle and the mobster

Vito Genovese weren't connected, but perhaps she was tired of explaining that there was more than one Genovese family.

"I got annoyed with them," she testified. "I said, 'Yeah, that's right. I take in thousands a day and I get five percent.' Next thing I knew, they dragged me in."

The patrolmen walked feisty Kitty to a squad car. They drove her to the precinct house, where she was booked and photographed: a tousle-haired twenty-six-year-old in a checkered blouse. She gave the police photographer a level gaze. There was a bit of twine visible on her collar. The twine held a plastic sign identifying Catherine S. Genovese, charged with bookmaking in August 1961. This is the image of Kitty that the world knows, her mug shot.

She and Dee Guarnieri were convicted and fined fifty dollars each. After losing her job at the Queens Café, Kitty went to work at Ev's 11th Hour.

T wo and a half years later, on the chilly morning of March 12, 1964, she unlocked Ev's front door and stepped inside. She locked the door behind her. Hollis was rougher than Kew Gardens. People in Hollis locked their doors.

She flipped the lights on and twisted the knob on a wall-mounted radiator that woke with a shudder. As heat began spreading through the bar, Kitty put away the mugs and highball glasses Horan had washed before closing the night before. She checked the beer taps, the bathrooms, the levels of her bottles of whiskey, gin, vodka, and the rest. When the barroom was in order, she went to a safe in Ev's office and retrieved the cash drawer for the register.

Then it was time to open up. "It wouldn't take long for the regulars to come in," Mary Ann recalls. "She had some who'd sit and drink all day and leave a dollar tip."

"Not a great-tips place," agrees Horan, "but we had our nights. You could make thirty dollars on a good shift." After 6:00 p.m., when he took over behind the bar, Kitty turned to her managerial duties: balancing the books, keeping inventory, filling out order forms. On busy nights she helped him serve drinks. By working double shifts she boosted her take-home pay to around $750 a month, worth about $5,000 in 2014 dollars. That was twice what Mary Ann earned at Club Chris, where she tended bar, and almost twice what Winston Moseley earned running a Remington Rand machine. When her father bugged her about getting married again, Kitty smiled and said, "I'm independent. No man could support me because I make more than a man."

As long as she didn't take vacations or make too many loans to customers and friends, she was on her way to making a down payment on the Italian restaurant she hoped to open someday. Sometimes she daydreamed about what the restaurant's name should be. Her gangsterish last name wouldn't work. Would she call the place *Kitty's*? Or *La Gattina*? That was Italian for "kitty."

That Thursday was "the usual," Horan recalls. With the Mets and Yanks training in Florida, there was no baseball on TV. The customers peered over their drinks at game shows, soap operas, and *I Love Lucy* reruns during the day. *The Munsters* came on after Horan arrived. *Perry Mason* started at nine, followed by *The Nurses*. The bar would be filling with regulars and drop-ins, the jukebox playing the Four Seasons, Sinatra, Johnny Cash, the ubiquitous Beatles, and the Kingsmen's goofy "Louie Louie," a tune so widely thought obscene that Hoover's FBI investigated it, only to rule that it was "unintelligible at any speed."

Six miles away, "I finished my shift at Club Chris and went bowling with Gloria Hominik," Mary Ann recalls. "Gloria was lovers with Kitty before I was. We all stayed friends." Mary Ann clinked beers with Gloria when one of them picked up a spare. After bowling and dinner she climbed the narrow stairs to their apartment. "It was three or four hours till Kitty got off work. I read a little. I remember I was reading *Let Us Now Praise Famous Men*—nonfiction, which was more her style. I read awhile and went to bed around eleven-thirty."

Business at Ev's slacked off around midnight, but the owner liked Kitty to keep the place open until three or four. It was now officially Friday, March 13, the anniversary of the night Kitty and Mary Ann met. Over the next hour a few drinkers who had been chased from other taverns came in, looking for a nightcap. Horan served all but the most blotto. He could handle cutting them off but often left that task to Kitty. She would say, "Honey, you've had enough." Smiling, but firm. She'd call a taxi if the drinker needed one, even pay for his ride home if it wasn't too far.

Kitty went out to eat with one of the regulars. There was apparently nothing romantic about their dinner, just a meal and a drink to occupy a couple of hours before closing time. She was back before three.

By then the place was empty. She told Horan he could close up a little early. "I'm going home," she said. "Goodnight, Vic."

It was thirty-four degrees outside, the street as cold and clear and shining as a mirror.

9

Night of the Hunt

He was awake and alert. Thinking. Lately his thoughts had been following particular tracks. Sex. Race. For all the lynchings, bombings, and freedom-rider beatings in the South, he thought, the North was just as bad in its way. Prejudice hid itself better in the North, where a black man had to be twice as smart and work twice as hard to keep up with white workers who might pretend to see him as an equal. Black women had it worse. Nobody seemed to care if they lived or died. Nobody noticed if they disappeared. White girls might be different though.

On weekend nights, he could smell Betty in the bed with him. Her scent aroused and disgusted him, particularly when she was having her period. But this was not a weekend night. It was a Thursday, and he was the only adult in the house on Sutter Avenue. Winston Moseley liked Thursday nights. He could skip sleep if he wanted, push through nine hours of work at Raygram the next day, and sleep in on Saturday. He thought of himself as an unlucky man, but nobody's unlucky about everything. When Moseley counted his blessings, one of them was that his wife worked nights.

That evening he had kissed Betty when she left for her night shift at Elmhurst Hospital after dinner. "I love you. You're perfect," he said. He often told Betty she was perfect, and believed it when he said it. Moseley loved his wife. Still he was glad when she drove off to work.

He fed the dogs, giving Wolfie a little extra. Later he tucked Mark and Kerry into bed and kissed them goodnight. He went to the kitchen and made himself a sandwich. The fridge was so full of six-packs of beer that there wasn't room for much else. He'd been drinking much more lately. He took his sandwich and a six-pack to the living room, where he sank into his favorite chair to drink and watch TV. *Perry Mason* was on. In tonight's all-white episode, "The Case of the Garrulous Go-Between," a girl secretly tapes her sessions with a fortune-teller who seems to know everything about her. When the girl's pet parrot and landlord turn up dead, Perry and Paul Drake solve the mystery.

After the news—Jimmy Hoffa sentenced to eight years in prison for jury tampering, Malcolm X breaking with the Nation of Islam, a Grammy to Allan Sherman for his funny song "Hello Mudduh, Hello Fadduh"—Johnny Carson welcomed the inevitable Dr. Joyce Brothers to the *Tonight Show*. Winston looked in on the boys, cozy in their beds. He was restless. He cracked open another beer. He may have watched a few minutes of the late movie, Eddie Albert in a thriller called *Orders to Kill*, before he armed himself and went outside to the Corvair. There was no need to lock up the house. With Wolfie and four other German shepherds inside, Moseley's house had to be one of the safest in the city.

Between 1:30 and 2:00 a.m., Moseley drove north through Jamaica and Hillside, then circled back toward South Ozone Park. He drove for more than an hour, just looking. He was accustomed to this kind of hunting. And he was willing to give up if it didn't work out. There had been other sleepless nights when he hunted successfully and got home safe with a secret no other living soul knew, and still others when he gave up, called it a night, and drove home. He knew how to wait.

Clouds obscured a thumbnail moon. At a few minutes to 3:00 he found himself in Hollis, heading east on Jamaica Avenue. He was thinking of turning back when a dark-haired young woman got into a red Fiat and drove off the other way. Moseley made a U-turn and followed her onto Grand Central Parkway. Her snub-nosed little car was five feet shorter and a thousand pounds lighter than his Corvair, but she drove flat-out. He had to step on the gas to keep up. She pulled off the parkway at the Queens Boulevard exit and turned left onto Austin Street.

"A quiet, dark street," he would call it. "It was what I was hoping for."

He followed the red Fiat to the Long Island Rail Road station. NO PARKING signs warned motorists away, but the locals knew better. The Fiat pulled into an open space while the dirty white Corvair continued for half a block. Moseley parked at a bus stop under bare-limbed trees. He pulled on a stocking cap and hurried toward the L.I.R.R. lot as the Fiat driver spent a few seconds locking her car.

Kitty turned toward the Tudor building, fifteen yards away. Kew Gardens was quiet. The drugstore and coffeehouse had closed hours ago. The second-floor apartment windows were dark. The door that led to her second-floor apartment was in back of the building, facing the railroad tracks. It was dark back there, but pale-yellow streetlamps lit the sidewalk on the Austin Street side of the building. Kitty must have sensed danger because she walked toward the lights. She may have hoped that Bailey's Pub was still open. She may have been thinking of the police-emergency callbox on a phone pole at the corner of Austin Street and Lefferts Boulevard.

She heard footsteps. She began to run. It was 3:19 a.m.

37 Who Saw Murder Didn't Call the Police
Apathy at Stabbing of Queens Woman Shocks Inspector

BY MARTIN GANSBERG

For more than half an hour 38 respectable, law-abiding citizens in Queens watched a killer stalk and stab a woman in three separate attacks in Kew Gardens.

Twice the sound of their voices and the sudden glow of their bedroom lights interrupted him and frightened him off. Each time he returned, sought her out and stabbed her again. Not one person telephoned the police during the assault; one witness called after the woman was dead. . . .

Assistant Chief Inspector Frederick M. Lussen, in charge of the borough's detectives and a veteran of 25 years of homicide investigations, is still shocked. He can give matter-of-fact recitation of many murders. But the Kew Gardens slaying baffles him—not because it is a murder, but because the "good people" failed to call the police.

"As we have reconstructed the crime," he said, "the assailant had three chances to kill this woman during a 35-minute period. He returned twice to complete the job. If we had been called when he first attacked, the woman might not be dead now."

This is what the police say happened beginning at 3:20 A.M. in the staid, middle-class, tree-lined Austin Street area:

Twenty-eight-year-old Catherine Genovese, who was called Kitty by almost everyone in the neighborhood, was returning home from her job as manager of a bar in Hollis. She parked her red Fiat in a lot adjacent to the Long Island Rail Road Station. . . .

Miss Genovese noticed a man at the far end of the lot. . . . She halted. Then, nervously, she headed up Austin Street toward Lefferts Boulevard, where there is a call box to the 102d Police Precinct in nearby Richmond Hill.

"HE STABBED ME!"

She got as far as a street light in front of a bookstore before the man grabbed her. She screamed. Lights went on. . . . Windows slid open and voices punctured the early-morning stillness.

Miss Genovese screamed, "Oh, my God, he stabbed me! Please help me! Please help me!"

From one of the upper windows, a man called down, "Let that girl alone!" The assailant looked up at him, shrugged and walked down Austin Street toward a white sedan parked a short distance away. Miss Genovese struggled to her feet. Lights went out. The killer returned to Miss Genovese, now trying to make her way around the side of the building to get to her apartment. The assailant stabbed her again.

"I'm dying!" she shrieked. "I'm dying!"

A CITY BUS PASSED

Windows were opened again, and lights went on in many apartments. The assailant got into his car and drove away. Miss Genovese staggered to her feet. A city bus, Q-10, passed. It was 3:35 A.M.

The assailant returned. By then, Miss Genovese had crawled to the back of the building, where the freshly painted brown doors to the apartment house held out hope of safety. The killer tried the first door; she wasn't there. At the second door, 82-62 Austin Street, he saw her slumped on the floor at the foot of the stairs. He stabbed her a third time—fatally.

It was 3:50 by the time the police received their first call, from a man who was a neighbor of Miss Genovese. In two minutes they were at the scene. The neighbor, a 70-year-old woman and another woman were the only persons on the street. Nobody else came forward.

The man explained that he had called the police after much deliberation. He had phoned a friend in Nassau County for advice and then he had crossed the roof of the building to the apartment of the elderly woman to get her to make the call.

"I didn't want to get involved," he sheepishly told the police. . . .

It was 4:25 A.M. when the ambulance arrived for the body of Miss Genovese. It drove off. "Then," a solemn police detective said, "the people came out."

At least that's what the newspaper said.

10

Postmortem

Somebody was pounding on the door. "It woke me up," Mary Ann says, "and I was scared. Who comes knocking at four in the morning?"

The police. Kitty had been attacked, they said. Stabbed. She was put in an ambulance to Queens General. She had lost a lot of blood. It didn't look good.

"I went numb." Mary Ann thought she might throw up. A police radio crackled. One of the policemen crowding her apartment said that Kitty had died on the way to the hospital.

By then every light was on, the building abuzz with activity. Radio calls had summoned the borough's Emergency Service Unit with its

Fingerprint and Photo Units. The specialists roped off the L.I.R.R. parking lot. Soon more than forty detectives, technicians, and patrolmen descended on the crime scene.

Karl Ross came by to keep Mary Ann company. Ross brought a bottle. Looking frazzled and hung over, he poured them each a glass of vodka. He spent the next three hours commiserating with Mary Ann while slowly draining the bottle, never mentioning what he had seen and heard outside his apartment a few hours before.

Detective Mitchell Sang arrived a little before seven in the morning. A broad-shouldered bulldog of a man, Sang had a slick-shaved head—rare enough to draw stares on the streets in those days. He was one of two detectives on duty at the 102nd Precinct when the emergency call came in. A girl stabbed. A homicide. Sang took an instant dislike to dog groomer Ross, who kept interrupting as he tried to question Mary Ann. According to Sang's boss, Deputy Inspector Albert Seedman, who reviewed Sang's report, Mary Ann was "shy and withdrawn . . . practically stone." Ross "claimed to be consoling her" while "swilling vodka and acting obnoxious," interfering with Sang's investigation.

Detective Sang knew something that Mary Ann didn't. He knew that Kitty had been attacked on the Austin Street side of the building and had been found on the opposite side of the building more than half an hour later, lying at the foot of the stairs that led to Ross's apartment.

"Why don't you go home?" he asked Ross. "I'll talk to you later."

Ross got testy. "If Mary Ann wants me to stay, I can stay," he said.

This was not the way to deal with Detective Mitch Sang on a cold, ugly morning when he had a murder on his plate, the first Kew Gardens murder in years. Sang yanked Ross out of his chair ("politely," in the chief's account), marched him downstairs, gave him a shove, and told him to get lost. The bullet-headed detective was on his way back up the stairs when he heard a noise behind him. He turned and saw that Ross had kicked a hole in the street-level door.

Sang hauled the yelping, cursing dog groomer to the precinct house, where Ross was booked for disorderly conduct, the first arrest related to the murder of Kitty Genovese.

Queens Homicide detectives John Carroll and Jerry Burns took over the case later that morning. They questioned more than a dozen of Kitty and Mary Ann's neighbors. They tracked down Angelo Lanzone and rousted bartender Victor Horan out of bed. Now they turned up the heat on Mary Ann.

"It was good cop, bad cop, but the bad one, Burns, did most of the talking," she says. Detective Burns, a jowly lawman with a resemblance to FBI Director Hoover, pressed for details: Where were you last night? How long have you known the deceased? Who were her friends? When was the last time you argued? Did you have sex problems? "I was still in shock. It took me a while to realize what he was getting at. They thought I might be the one who killed her."

The police had talked to enough friends and neighbors to know that Kitty and Mary Ann were lovers. Burns asked about their past affairs, their sex life, their sexual positions. The longer he went on, the more his interrogation felt like a vice raid in her own apartment. "I didn't want to talk to the cops, especially not him," Mary Ann recalls. "But they harassed me for six hours, trying to get me to say something bad about Kitty. How professional was that? For the police? Finally they got me to admit it—okay, we were lesbians."

Almost fifty years later, Mary Ann's memory of her "confession" brings tears to her eyes. "I was upset with myself for revealing that. I've always regretted it. What right did they have to know?"

Deputy Inspector Seedman, who would be promoted to chief of detectives for the three-thousand-detective New York City Police Department after overseeing the Genovese case, thought it mattered. In his view, "One of the most common motives for murder is jealousy. It's also our experience that homosexual romances produce more jealousy by far than 'straight' romances. More jealousy means more chance for violence. Women, in fact, can be more possessive toward their lovers than men." That made Mary Ann the prime suspect. As Seedman recalled in his lurid 1974 memoir, *Chief!*, Kitty's murder "appeared at first not to be much different from a thousand other knifings in a city full of blades." He was exaggerating: there had been 548 homicides in New York City the year before, giving the nation's largest city a lower murder rate than Chicago and Miami. Almost half of those 548 homicides occurred in Manhattan. Queens was safer, and quiet Kew Gardens was among the safest neighborhoods in Queens. A Kew Gardens murder was news. But it wasn't yet big news. At first, no newspaper or radio station presented Kitty's death as anything more than a police-blotter entry. Several morning papers carried brief items on Saturday, March 14. The *Times'* unsigned notice ran 126 words: "A 28-year-old Queens woman was stabbed to death early yesterday morning outside her apartment house in Kew Gardens. Neighbors who were awakened by her screams found the woman, Miss Catherine Genovese of 82-70 Austin Street, shortly after 3 A.M. . . . The police, who spent the day searching for the murder weapon, interviewing witnesses and checking automobiles that had been seen in the neighborhood, said last night they had no clues."

The detectives drove Mary Ann to the morgue at Queens General Hospital, where she identified Kitty's body. "That was hard." She remembers the sight of her lover on a stainless-steel gurney, a white sheet pulled up to Kitty's pointy chin, hiding her wounds.

"Yes, that's her," Mary Ann told the police.

Afterward, she sat on a bench outside the morgue. The cops offered to drive her home, "but I didn't want to leave her there alone." Finally she stood and started for the glass doors at the end of the hall.

Queens medical examiner William Benenson performed Kitty's autopsy. The decedent was identified as Catherine Genovese W-F-28, DOA at QGH, Queens General Hospital. Benenson found "thirteen stab wounds scattered over the body, nine in front and four in the back . . . a stab wound in the throat . . . several slashes on the right hand." The stab wounds were "oblique and jagged," suggesting that the victim twisted, trying to avoid each thrust of the knife. "There were cuts on the fingers, defense cuts. She had her hands up." Trying to fight her attacker. She had bled profusely, but the cause of death was bilateral pneumothorax, which means that air escaping from Kitty's punctured lungs filled her chest cavity, compressing the lungs. She suffocated, still trying to speak.

Mary Ann spent much of the weekend after the murder drinking with Karl Ross. Afraid to be alone after Ross padded back to his apartment, she asked Angelo Lanzone to sleep over. Lanzone slept on the sofa-bed in the living room. "It didn't help. I still woke up yelling," Mary Ann says. The police kept coming around to ask leering questions. After hours of quizzing her about her lesbian love life with Kitty, they wanted to know if she was sleeping with Lanzone.

Neighbors shied away from Mary Ann. Detectives Burns, Carroll, and Sang had questioned them about Kitty and Mary Ann and their "fast crowd," which was cop code for "gay crowd." Lesbian friends began hanging up the phone when Mary Ann called. "I can't blame them," she says today. "Gay people were paranoid enough already. Now they've got the police asking questions. Did they know us? Did they sleep with us? My friends all stopped talking to me. They thought they were being watched. They thought their phones were tapped."

She drank herself to sleep and woke shouting in the middle of the night. Lanzone tried to help. "I kept her company right through the funeral," he recalls. "Which didn't go so well."

Kitty's parents arranged for a funeral Mass followed by her burial at Lakeview Cemetery in New Canaan, forty wooded acres wedged between Norwalk Harbor and the I-95 freeway. Rachel Genovese could barely stay on her feet. Her husband and four surviving children had kept the worst details from her; all Rachel knew was that some-body had stabbed her daughter to death. "My mother couldn't handle it," Kitty's brother Vincent said. "We read about it in the papers, the gruesome description," and they threw the papers away. Mary Ann would have liked to comfort Rachel, but the family kept her away. They didn't want her in the front row at the funeral. The Genoveses had always tried to be kind when Kitty brought her lover to their home, but now that Kitty was gone, they didn't want Mary Ann making some sort of lesbian scene at the cemetery.

After the funeral Mary Ann went back to her empty bed. She fed and talked to Andrew, the poodle Kitty had bought her as a peace offering, until Kitty's father came and took the dog to Connecticut. Mary Ann spent hours drinking with Ross, both of them grumbling about the police. Ross said they'd fined him twenty-five dollars for kicking a hole in the door downstairs. Disturbing the peace. They were nasty, he said, asking questions about the night Kitty died as if he had something to do with it.

Buzzed on more liquor than she was used to, Mary Ann heard Ross without really listening. Had she listened better, she might have connected the dots between his complaints about nasty cops asking questions and the questions themselves, legitimate questions about the crime scene at 82-62 Austin Street, three doors down from Kitty and Mary Ann's door—Karl Ross's address.

Later that week, without telling her, the police took Mary Ann's name off their list of suspects. Now they had none. They had no murder weapon, no suspects, no leads. Then, on the afternoon of March 18, five days after the murder, a Corona man named Raoul Cleary saw a skinny Negro carrying a TV set out of a neighbors' house.

"What are you doing in the Bannisters' house?" Cleary asked.

"It's okay, I'm helping them move," the man said.

Cleary watched him stow the TV in a white Corvair and saunter back to the Bannister house, so casually he was actually whistling. While he was inside, Cleary phoned a neighbor.

"Are the Bannisters moving?"

"Absolutely not," the friend said. "I'm calling the police."

After watching from his window and seeing no sign of the intruder, Cleary went to the Corvair at the curb. He opened its hood, pulled off the distributor cap, slammed the hood shut, and retreated to his apartment to wait and watch.

The slim Negro reappeared, empty-handed this time. When his car wouldn't start, he got out and strolled away. He was in no hurry; he didn't run even when patrolmen Daniel Dunn and Pete Williamson, responding to the phone call from Cleary's friend, pulled up beside him in their squad car. Dunn and Williamson frisked the suspect and found a screwdriver in his pocket. Returning to search his car, they found the Bannisters' television in the Corvair's trunk, as well as another TV set, a few small appliances, and a stash of porno-graphic pictures and magazines. Asked his name, the man said, "Winston Moseley." Moseley was arrested—thanks to two neighbors who saw a crime and got involved.

At the 114th Precinct station house in Astoria, Detective John Tartaglia interviewed the burglar. Moseley sat with his hands in his lap, calm as a housecat. Tartaglia, a methodical thirteen-year vet-eran with a basso profundo voice, noted his "calm and gentleness." The detective had no reason to see this young family man with a steady job and no arrest record as anything but a petty crook. "What's your story, Moseley?" he asked.

Speaking in a monotone, Moseley admitted stealing the TVs and appliances. He said he'd pulled off dozens of similar jobs in the past year, usually between midnight and sunup. He'd give the TVs to his father, who had a repair shop in Corona. As for the dirty pictures, described by Patrolman Dunn as "thirty photographs depicting nude males and females in obscene, indecent and filthy poses; and forty magazines depicting pictures of nude females," Moseley had a ready explanation. He said the porn was part of his haul from an earlier burglary. "I'd never buy that stuff myself."

Tartaglia's next step was to drive the burglar to his father's shop on Northern Boulevard, where the detective arrested Alphonso Mose-ley for receiving stolen property. Neither of the Moseley men showed the slightest emotion. In the deputy inspector's report, Alphonso was "gray-haired and dignified, ruled by the same sense of calm as his son." Still there was something in Winston Moseley's blank expression that made Tartaglia think he wasn't telling the whole truth. That afternoon, in a second sit-down at the station house, Tartaglia announced that he was going to hold Moseley a little longer, to ask him about more than a bunch of stolen blenders and TVs. He wanted to talk about some other things that had been going on lately in

Queens. Unsolved things. Starting with the murder of Kitty Genovese. Some of the witnesses reported seeing a white car at the crime scene, a car that might have been a Corvair. What did Moseley think about that?

Moseley said nothing. Tartaglia could have let it go. After all there were no signs that this petty thief had any violence in him. Tartaglia could have cut Moseley loose to face a burglary charge that would likely get a first offender like him probation or a suspended sentence. But something bugged him about this fellow. The longer they talked, the more Tartaglia sensed what Chief Seedman would later call "something creepy in his expressionless calm."

Detective John Carroll of Queens Homicide and Detective Mitch Sang, the bald bulldog from the 102nd Precinct, stood in the squad room at the 114th, smoking cigars. They joined the interrogation. None of the detectives informed the suspect of his right to remain silent or to have a lawyer present. This would become an issue later, when Moseley claimed that he should have been fully informed of his rights. The Supreme Court wouldn't decide *Miranda v. Arizona*, the case requiring police to tell suspects their rights, for another two years. Had his case played out differently, with Moseley pressing the issue from the start, there is a chance that police would have gone on to read countless arrestees their "Moseley rights" in subsequent years. But such an alternate history probably wouldn't have changed what came next. He was ready to talk.

After a few minutes, Carroll reached for the suspect's hands. He held them up to the fluorescent light. There were small scabs on two of Moseley's fingers.

"I scratched them working around the house," Moseley said.

Carroll wasn't buying it. "No," he said. "You got those cuts from Kitty Genovese when you were putting the knife in."

In Seedman's account, "The room filled with silence. . . . Moseley looked around almost shyly, a bare curl of a smile shaping on his lips. It was 5:57. 'Okay, I killed her,' he said."

Saying it seemed to relax him. Speaking as if he were describing an ordinary evening, he told the detectives how he had gone for a drive on the night of March 12 with a serrated hunting knife in his coat pocket. How he spotted Kitty getting into her Fiat on Jamaica Avenue in Hollis and followed her to Kew Gardens, where he jumped her, killed her, and made his escape.

The detectives weren't sure they believed him. They needed details. They kept him talking, and soon he mentioned something that only the killer was likely to know. "She was wearing a sanitary pad." Mary Ann and the medical examiner were the only others who knew Kitty was menstruating.

Later that evening, after more than eight hours of questioning, Moseley asked for dinner. "I'd like a double hamburger, coffee light with no sugar, and a piece of French apple pie." When the food arrived he resumed his confession, saying, "I don't mind talking while I eat." He added other details no one else could have known, mentioning the brown billfold he had stolen—Kitty's Christmas present from Mary Ann. He said he had taken out forty-nine dollars, then tossed the billfold into the weeds by the Raygram parking lot when he went to work later that morning. Sure enough, detectives found the billfold in the weeds.

Moseley added a last fillip to his account. He'd been driving home after killing Kitty, he said—it must have been a little after 4:00 a.m.—when he came upon a car idling at a green light. The driver had fallen asleep. Moseley parked, and with the bloodstained hunting knife still in his pocket he approached the other car. He tapped on the sleeping motorist's window. The man woke, blinked, rolled down his window.

"Listen, mister," Moseley said. "You shouldn't be sleeping like that. The carbon monoxide builds up. Or somebody could come along and do something bad to you."

The man thanked him. "You're right. You're a good fella."

Moseley returned to the Corvair. He drove home, washed Kitty's blood off the knife, and sat up until the phone rang at seven—his wife calling from the hospital to wake him up. Then he fed the dogs and went to work.

While his confession left little doubt that Winston Moseley had killed Kitty Genovese, the quiet killer had other surprises for Seedman's detective squad. During later interrogations he admitted to still more burglaries, several rapes, and another murder. His stories checked out. Police found some of the stolen TVs and other appliances at Alphonso's shop. Moseley went on to say that he had brutally attacked several young Negro women without attracting any attention from the police, and claimed he had killed one of them, a young housewife in South Ozone Park. The detectives recalled that murder because it had been particularly gruesome. The victim's name was Annie Mae Johnson. She was twenty-four. Her body was found riddled with puncture wounds and partly burned. The crime was unsolved.

According to Moseley, he had gone out for a drive on a snowy night twelve days before he killed Kitty. Seeing a woman parking her car on 133rd Avenue in South Ozone Park, a few blocks from his house, he parked behind her, jumped out, and pressed a short-barreled .22 rifle to her belly. Annie Mae Johnson, terrified, tried to hand him her purse. He took it, then shot her. As Moseley told the Queens detectives, his rifle was "one of those single-action .22s. You have to reload it after every shot. She held out her keys to me while I reloaded. She said, 'Please help me get into my house.'" Shot once, kneeling, she reached toward him. He helped her up, then shot her again, "three, maybe four times." In his affectless voice, he described rolling his victim into her house. "I tried to drag her, but she was hard to handle. I had to roll her in. I undressed her, then I had relations with her."

As he did with his wife, he began with cunnilingus. "Then I lay on top of her." Unable to maintain his erection, he yanked Annie Mae Johnson's scarf off her neck. She was still breathing. Frustrated and angry, Moseley scouted around the house, searching cabinets and drawers, until he found a book of matches. He covered her body with wadded-up newspapers. He set the papers on fire, stuffed the scarf between her legs, and lit the scarf to make sure that her crotch burned. Then he drove home to his family.

The detectives weren't sure what to think of this second confession. Most of the details matched the evidence. Could this whispery little business-machine operator really have gone on a spree of burglaries, rapes, and murders as a sideline?

Queens assistant district attorney Phil Chetta, a hard-charging young prosecutor born and raised in Corona, doubted it. Yes, it would be great to solve two murders at once. Yes, Moseley seemed to know things that no innocent man could know. But for Chetta those affirmatives added up to a negative because one big piece of the puzzle didn't fit: Annie Mae Johnson hadn't been shot. The coroner's report was clear on that.

Now several detectives erupted at once. According to Seedman they barked at the suspect: "Goddamn! You lie, Moseley! She was stabbed with a fucking ice pick! You lied to us about Genovese too, didn't you?"

Moseley shrugged. In Seedman's account he sat quietly, "with the knowing look of a teacher waiting patiently for his perplexed class to catch on to a problem he has given them." The coroner was wrong, he said. "I shot her."

There was one way to test his story. Annie Mae Johnson, slain in Queens, had been buried in a family plot in Monck's Corner, South Carolina. Two weeks after her funeral, Seedman and the department brass approved an exhumation. On March 20 three gravediggers hauled her pine coffin out of the red Carolina clay. South Carolina coroners working with the New York detectives used an X-ray machine borrowed from the South Carolina Medical College in Charleston to reexamine the body. The X-rays showed raisin-shaped dots in the victim's stomach—six .22 caliber bullets. The Queens coroner had mistaken small-caliber bullet wounds for the punctures made by an ice pick.

Now the police were sure they had the man who'd slain Annie Mae Johnson and Kitty Genovese. Unfortunately for them, he wasn't done confessing.

Moseley was sitting in the interview room, looking smug as ever, when one of the cops screwed up. As a Queens prosecutor recalled the crucial instant, "Suddenly, without thinking, one of the detectives recklessly blurted out, 'I bet you also killed that fifteen-year-old girl last year.'"

He meant Barbara Kralik, murdered in Springfield Gardens, Queens, three miles from Kew Gardens, in July 1963.

Moseley said, "Yeah, I did that one, too."

Assistant DA Chetta couldn't believe this was happening. The Kralik case was a layup! The killer was Alvin "the Monster" Mitchell, a preening, pompadoured young thug whose confession matched every detail of the crime. As far as Chetta was concerned, Monster Mitchell was as good as convicted of first-degree murder. The last thing prosecutors needed was a false confession to throw doubt on the real one.

"*Definitely,*" Moseley continued. "I killed her, too."

Chetta thought Moseley was sharp for a lowlife—maybe he was trying to set up an insanity defense by confessing to murders he didn't commit. Next thing you know he'll say he shot Kennedy.

The furious Chetta, cut off any further questioning of suspect Moseley, but he was too late. The news leaked, and on March 22 the *Daily News* revealed Moseley's and Mitchell's dueling confessions in a story headed TWO ADMIT SAME SLAYING, BAFFLE COPS. The *Daily News* reported that Moseley knew details that only Kralik's killer could have known. That was false, but Chetta had no choice: he put the Kralik case on hold. With the newspapers following every move he made, the assistant DA knew that one slip in any of three murder cases—Barbara Kralik, Annie Mae Johnson, Kitty Genovese—might sink all of them. Chetta needed help from above.

11

Neighbors

Abraham Michael Rosenthal, forty-one, was a dark-haired, bespectacled ringer for Clark Kent. He had risen from humble beginnings in the Bronx, writing his first stories for the *New York Times* while still a student at City College, and won a Pulitzer Prize in 1960 for his reporting from Eastern Europe. Now, as the *Times'* newly minted city editor, the bubbly, still-boyish Rosenthal intended to make the paper's local coverage as strong as its international reportage. "The Khyber Pass was my kind of story," he wrote. "I pride myself on being a different breed of newspaperman than that old police reporter—traveled and socially conscious." As part of his mission he cultivated local leaders like police commissioner Michael Murphy.

In Rosenthal's words, Murphy "looks like a tough Irish cop because he is a tough Irish cop." Three years after joining a proud blue line of New York City Police Department bosses that included Theodore Roosevelt, the six-foot, 200-pound commissioner was sometimes called Bull Murphy. He joined Rosenthal for lunch at Emil's, a restaurant near City Hall known for sauerbraten and dumplings, on the day after the *Daily News'* TWO ADMIT SAME SLAYING story. Ten days had passed since Kitty died. As Rosenthal recalled their lunch, the commissioner "sits always with his back to the wall, an old police habit, and orders shrimp curry and rice." Rosenthal had come to lunch with an agenda—the dueling confessions in the Kralik case intrigued him—but he kept his thoughts to himself as the meal progressed. He wrote later, "Murphy did not have murder on his mind that day. In the spring of 1964, what was usually on the mind of the Police Commissioner of New York was the haunting fear that someday blood would flow in the streets because of the tensions of the civil rights movement." That fear was about to come true. Four months later one of Murphy's officers would shoot and kill a black fifteen-year-old, James Powell, triggering a week of race riots in Harlem and Bedford-Stuyvesant. Those riots helped trigger others in Philadelphia, Chicago, and northern New Jersey. Nineteen sixty-five would bring internecine battle between black separatist leaders that triggered Malcolm X's assassination in New York's Audubon Ballroom in February. Six months later, riots torched much of Watts in Los Angeles, making "Burn, baby, burn" a slogan for angry slum-dwellers from Watts to the Bronx. Racial friction threatened to set off race war in the tinderbox of Commissioner Murphy's five boroughs, a threat that would escalate for the rest of the decade, but Rosenthal was wrong about the commissioner's preoccupations that day at Emil's. Murphy may have been dreading race riots, but he also had murder on his mind.

They were ordering coffee when Rosenthal asked a question he had saved for a casual moment. "How about that double confession out in Queens?" he asked. "What's that all about?"

Murphy didn't bite. Multiple confessions could only embarrass the department. So he changed the subject. He said, "Brother, that Queens story is one for the books. Thirty-eight witnesses." He was talking about the Kitty Genovese case.

"Thirty-eight?" Rosenthal asked.

"Thirty-eight," the commissioner said. "I've been in this business a long time, but this beats everything."

Rosenthal felt a spark running up and down the back of his neck, the spine-tingling sense that he was onto a story readers would never forget. "I'd like to assign a reporter," he told Commissioner Murphy. Their meetings were understood to be off the record, but Murphy agreed to cooperate. Why not—this was the outcome he wanted. To top it off, he had a patrolman drive the editor uptown to the *Times* building in a police car.

That afternoon, Rosenthal summoned reporter Martin Gansberg to his office. While waiting at his two-ton desk in the middle of the newsroom, Rosenthal pondered the Genovese story. The *Times*, *Post*, *Daily News*, *Herald Tribune*, and *Newsday* had all covered Kitty's murder. The *Herald Tribune* had even captured the crime's lonely poignance in an article headed *"HELP" CRY IGNORED, GIRL DIES OF KNIFING*. "The neighbors had grandstand seats for the slaying of Kitty Genovese," wrote reporter Robert Parrella, working off the initial police reports. "And yet, when the pretty, diminutive 28-year-old brunette called for help, she called in vain." But the *Herald Tribune* buried Parrella's story at the bottom of page ten. The other papers treated it as little more than a police-blotter item. Only Rosenthal, with a little prodding from Commissioner Murphy, saw its potential.

"People doing nothing about a murder—even if there were only eight or nine or so—was obviously a story," Rosenthal wrote later. "Thirty-eight was impossible, I knew."

Abe Rosenthal knew he was the man to interpret this story. He had grown up in the Bronx, the only son of a house painter who had given up a life he loved in Canada to raise his children in New York. Harry Rosenthal, a rabbi's son born in Belarus, had changed the family name from Shipiatski upon emigrating to Canada in the 1890s. To him, *Rosenthal* sounded Canadian enough. Harry was an outdoorsman. He worked on the railroad. He worked as a forester and fur trapper. When the Depression brought logging and trapping to a standstill, he took his wife and six children—five daughters plus Abe, the sickly baby—to the Bronx, where Harry painted houses and dreamed of the forests of Ontario, where he belonged. One day he was painting an upper floor when he fell from a scaffold. His injuries slowly killed him. His son Abe, a star public-school student who walked on crutches owing to a bone infection, cast his crutches aside after the new sulfa drugs cured him, only to see one of his beloved sisters die of pneumonia. That left him with four older sisters. One died after giving birth. Two more died of cancer long before their brilliant, scrappy little brother won the Pulitzer Prize. Abe Rosenthal seldom went a day without thinking of his father and dead sisters, resolving to honor their memories with his work at America's greatest newspaper.

Rosenthal believed in the American promise, which others called the American dream. He believed that he had proved it to be real: a failed fur-trapper's son had risen to the post of metropolitan editor of the *New York Times*! Perhaps as a function of his worldview, which became the *Times'* cityview under his aegis, stories that came across the city desk might run or not run, or be played more or less prominently, depending on their resonance to Rosenthal. As Gay Talese put it in his 1966 portrait of the paper, *The Kingdom and the Power,*

"Rosenthal wanted to touch the nerve of New York." And he might be willing to cut a few minor corners if that's what it took. Veteran reporters "became resentful," Talese wrote, "and helped to spread the word that the new policy was to 'fake' stories and overdramatize events." They joked about the time when Rosenthal, then an ambitious young correspondent in India, traveled fifteen hundred miles to file a story he'd already finished, so that the piece could be datelined *At the Khyber Pass.*

City-desk reporters knew that Rosenthal expected who-what-when-where accuracy, but most of all he prized stories that packed an emotional punch.

Martin Gansberg was an unlikely choice to cover a murder in Queens. Brooklyn-born Gansberg, forty-two, had been news editor of the *Times'* international edition before shifting to the city desk as a reporter. He and Rosenthal had joined the paper at about the same time and competed as they advanced. Rosenthal's desk and title showed him to be the winner on that score. A year younger than Gansberg, he claimed later that he had selected his onetime rival partly for his inexperience: Gansberg was "new enough not to resent dogged difficult work that might turn to nothing." He cited another reason for assigning Marty Gansberg to the Genovese murder: as the editor scanned the busy newsroom, Rosenthal recalled, "he was within my line of vision."

The moment Gansberg reached his desk, Rosenthal told him what he had learned from Commissioner Murphy. "I want you to go out to Kew Gardens," he said.

Newsroom lore has the eager reporter hurrying to the elevator while Rosenthal cries, "Gansberg, get that story!" The line sounds too pulpy to be true, more like something Clark Kent's boss, Perry White, would shout. All Rosenthal recalled was asking, "Marty, would you mind taking a look at this thing?"

Gansberg spent three days interviewing witnesses, neighbors, and cops. His legwork helped recast the story. Until then the Kitty Genovese murder had been a brief notice in respectable papers and the tacky tale of a barmaid's demise in a few tabloids. Gansberg's account of thirty-eight bad Samaritans changed everything. The *Times* gave it four columns on the front page on March 27, two weeks after the crime. It is likely that editor Rosenthal wrote the dramatic opener: "For more than half an hour 38 respectable, law-abiding citizens in Queens watched a killer stalk and stab a woman in three separate attacks in Kew Gardens."

Under the banner of the world's leading news source, the *New York Times* at the height of its influence, a two-week-old story became a sensation. Newspapers in England, Russia, Japan, and the Middle East picked it up. As recast by Rosenthal and Gansberg, Kitty's murder had irresistible elements of noir fiction: a gritty urban setting, craven bystanders, a defenseless young woman. In New York, the *Post, Daily News,* and *Herald Tribune* seized on the story with renewed gusto. One newspaper reader blamed Kitty's plight on the deadening effects of television: thirty-eight passive viewers, numbed by sex and violence on TV, turning away as if they were switching channels. Another blamed the women's-lib movement: militant females had turned men off, killing chivalry. A minister claimed that Kitty's killing proved that American society was "as sick as the one that crucified Jesus." Mike Wallace narrated a CBS radio think piece, "The Apathetic American," lamenting urban isolation and anomie. *Life* magazine's Loudon Wainwright, en route to Kew Gardens to cover the suddenly newsworthy trial of Winston Moseley, accused his fellow Americans of being "a callous, chickenhearted and immoral people." Kitty's murder had "lacerated the consciences of people all over the United States," wrote Wainwright. On one hand the crime stirred something primal: the ur-terror of being alone in the dark when a predator strikes. At the same time Kitty's story seemed as modern as the vivid hues on a color TV. In urban America in the '60s you might have a thousand neighbors only to die alone while they stood by their windows, watching.

Rosenthal was pleased with the story's impact. He could live with glitches like a headline reading *37 WHO SAW MURDER DIDN'T CALL THE POLICE* over a story that put the number at thirty-eight. There were other errors too, but nobody noticed them. What stuck in the public mind was the heartless indifference of modern Americans, particularly in New York, more particularly in Kew Gardens, home of at least thirty-seven bad Samaritans. Or was it thirty-eight?

"**W**e always loved our little village," recalls Murray Berger. He and his wife, Carol, moved to Kew Gardens as newlyweds in 1957.

"A quiet little town fifteen minutes from Manhattan," says Carol Berger, sitting beside her husband of fifty-six years. The Bergers have now lived around the corner from the murder scene for more than half a century.

"A place where you left your doors unlocked."

"But then, Kitty Genovese."

"It wasn't just the murder," Carol says. "It was later, when the *Times* story came out. That's what made Kitty front-page news."

"Literally," Murray says.

"After that we had an endless stream of reporters. Reporters and psychologists. Oh, they had a field day. They'd ring your doorbell. They'd stop you on the street. 'Did you know her? What was she like? Why didn't you do something?'"

"We *didn't* know her. We knew the block where she lived. That noisy bar—"

"Sometimes you'd hear people scream and yell."

"A domestic dispute, a couple drunks fighting, who knows? Who runs outside to find out?"

"*You* did," says Carol. "After the story came out, Murray would hear a noise in the night and run outside in his pajamas: '*Does somebody need help?*'"

"That story gave us all such a black eye," Murray says. "The world thought Kew Gardens was a terrible place."

"People moved out, especially the ones who lived near the scene. A lot of those apartments went empty. Who wants to live in a place like that? It was as if it was haunted."

Karl Ross moved out. He moved out West, people said, and disappeared. Mary Ann moved out after reporters spent the end of March and much of April chasing her down Austin Street. "Hounding me, yelling questions," she says. "'How do you feel?' Well, how do you *think* I felt?" She felt bad. Guilty, even. Guilty for sleeping through the attack that killed Kitty, and guilty for being alive. For weeks she hid in the apartment, still full of Kitty's things. Karl Ross came by "and we drank vodka all day." Finally Mary Ann joined the exodus. She rented a room in Far Rockaway, at the end of the subway line that ran through Queens to the chilly beach beyond the airport. She would open all the windows and listen to the surf. Using a photo for reference, she went back to working on her portrait of Kitty sitting on a park bench. "I never went back to Kew Gardens," she says, "except for the trial."

At his arraignment at the Queens County courthouse in Kew Gardens, two and a half blocks from the crime scene, Moseley stared at a gold star carved into the polished bench of Judge Bernard

Dubin, who read the charges against him. Burglary. Homicide: the murder of Annie Mae Johnson. Homicide: the murder of Kitty Genovese.

Betty Moseley, looking stricken, stood in the gallery in her white-on-white nurse's uniform while Judge Dubin shook his head at the ugliness of the crimes before him. "Two girls are dead, stark dead, because of a maniac roving the streets," the judge said. With a nod toward the reporters and spectators in his packed courtroom, he praised Commissioner Murphy's police department. "Reading the papers, you read about people downgrading the New York City Police Department, the finest department in the whole world. If it weren't for these policemen, these streets would be another Vietnam. These murders happened recently. You all read about them, and everyone's heart was broken. Girls and women were afraid to walk the streets. Some of them feel it's safer to walk in the wilderness with wild animals."

Peering down at the defendant, the judge banged his gavel. "Take him away. Bail is denied." Thus began Winston Moseley's imprisonment. It would last far longer than he thought he deserved, with one brief, bizarre interruption.

In April 1964 the Criminal Court of Queens County appointed Sidney Sparrow to represent Moseley. The son of a one-armed *Daily News* deliveryman, Sparrow, fifty-one, had risen to the top rank of the city's defense lawyers. An amateur artist, pilot, and scuba diver, Sparrow was a theatrical speaker with a bulbous nose that cast a shadow over his salt-and-pepper mustache. Court-watchers liked to say that he entered the courthouse with keys, handkerchief, and jurors in his pocket. "Jurors *liked* him," a colleague recalls. "Sometimes that was enough to win a case."

His defense team included three younger attorneys, Martha Zelman, Julius Lipitz, and Sparrow's son Bob. They all knew that Sparrow senior would be the star of the show when the murder trial opened in June. If anyone could deliver Moseley from Old Sparky, the electric chair at Sing Sing, it was the man other lawyers sometimes called El Sid.

The trial was on a fast track. Reforms following the 1966 *Miranda* ruling would usher in an era of defendant-friendly laws that slowed capital cases until they took years or even decades to litigate, but in 1964 a murderer could still be caught, tried, and executed in a matter of months. Queens County Indictment 542-64, *The People of the State of New York against Winston Moseley*, would be gaveled to life two and a half months after the crime.

The defendant was "*very* intelligent," Bob Sparrow recalls, "and very strange." During conferences with his legal team Moseley's emotionless voice never wavered as he described one hideous crime or another. "He knew an insanity defense was his only chance, but he refused to act crazy. That wasn't his style. He made it clear that nobody was going to tell him what to do."

The court commissioned a series of psychiatric examinations. Some tended to bolster the insanity defense Sidney Sparrow was planning to mount. One psychologist pronounced Moseley a paranoid schizophrenic with "a marked hostility toward women." Another noted his ability to wall himself off from his feelings, calling him "psychologically very well defended." A third psychologist was prepared to testify that the defendant suffered from a defect in reasoning that prevented him from knowing that there was anything wrong with killing people.

One recording of Moseley's pretrial interviews survives: a wrinkly reel of brown magnetic tape on a plastic spool. The tape went unplayed for decades. To get it started, you have to give the spool a push. Then comes a gummy foghorn sound that resolves into a voice as the tape speeds up, a plummy voice from the spring of 1964 asking, "Are you telling the truth?"

"Yes." Moseley's voice is a flat line.

"Because you want to explain or defend yourself?"

"I'm telling you because you asked me."

"You're not making a clean breast because of remorse?"

"No."

"How did you learn about the crimes you committed?"

"I read all the stories in the *Daily News* and the *Long Island Press*, the only two papers I read." Moseley's monosyllables could be spoken by a machine, but in a few longer answers his voice takes on the soft, lilting cadence of singer Nat King Cole. Asked about the upcoming World's Fair, he says, "My father has a television shop near there."

"Now, in the Genovese case, you put the hunting knife into her vaginal tract, didn't you?"

"Yes."

"Did you plunge the knife as deeply as you could?"

"Yes. To the handle, yes."

"Did you feel any compassion?"

"No."

Asked what he likes in life, Moseley mentions baseball and dogs. "Dogs love you regardless," he says.

"And people?"

"People are not like that. People remind me of flies. You know how they fly around out of reach, and then one comes just close enough for you to swat it."

Sparrow and his defense team spent weeks poring over psychiatric reports, underlining helpful phrases like "defect in reasoning" and discussing which psychologists would make the best witnesses. They interviewed and re-interviewed their client during the run-up to the trial. After one long day of hearing the calm, seemingly sensible Winston Moseley describe, over and over, what he had done to Kitty, one of Sparrow's assistants stood up, walked outside to the curb, and vomited.

Assistant District Attorney Frank Cacciatore must have wished that the public had never heard of Kitty Genovese. By casting her neighbors as monsters, the *Times'* dramatic account triggered low-level paranoia in Kew Gardens. Kitty's neighbors, all of them white, couldn't see why they should be blamed for a crime committed by a black man from Ozone Park. Many Kew Gardens residents were suspicious or fearful of the police in the first place, clamming up at the sight of a badge. Some were aging immigrants from Europe who had fled the Holocaust and dreaded any knock at the door. Other immigrants spoke little English. Still other Kew Gardeners had been pressed by so many policemen, reporters, and amateur and professional psychologists that they were just sick of answering questions.

Charles Skoller, the second-seat prosecutor assisting Cacciatore on the case, had mixed feelings about the *Times'* front-page story. Despite its errors, "the article did vividly describe Kitty's screams during the first attack and the indifference of her neighbors," recalled Skoller, who wrote a memoir, *Twisted Confessions*, about the Genovese and Kralik murders. He and the rest of Cacciatore's team spent April and May 1964 interviewing eyewitnesses and earwitnesses. Many had already told their stories to detectives, newsmen, and Sparrow's defense lawyers as well as friends, neighbors, and relatives. According to Skoller, "We asked two basic questions: What did you hear? What did you see?" Within days of starting work on the case, the prosecution team had doubts about the now-famous number thirty-eight. Thirty-eight was the number of people the police considered witnesses in the days following the crime. It was the number Commissioner Murphy cited over lunch at Emil's, the number that shocked editor Rosenthal, *Times* readers, and the world. Martin Gansberg had followed up on the work Murphy's detectives did, but neither Gansberg nor anyone else spent time ferreting out the source of the official number. The number thirty-eight came from the police; that was enough. Nobody identified the thirty-eight witnesses or counted the witnesses in the detectives' reports.

The prosecutors believed there may have been forty or fifty neighbors who heard Kitty's cries that night. But how many were half-asleep? How many rolled over and forgot what they heard? How many went to their windows but couldn't be sure what they were seeing? How many paced their apartments, wondering what to do, and then returned to their windows and saw nothing but an empty street?

By Skoller's count, no more than five or six neighbors saw and heard enough to know that Kitty was in mortal danger. Two of them would need to be kept off the witness stand. "Those two were sickening men. They knew Kitty was being killed," recalls Myrna Skoller, the assistant prosecutor's widow, "and they did nothing. But you can't let people like that testify in a murder trial because it might distract the jury. The jury might blame them instead of the real killer."

One of the "sickening men," Joseph Fink, worked as assistant superintendent of the Mowbray apartment tower across Austin Street from the Tudor building. Fink worked nights, running the elevator for tenants and guests. His seat in the Mowbray's lobby gave him a clear view of the sidewalk on the night Kitty died. The prosecutors interviewed him in April.

"Yeah, I saw it," he told them. From his vantage point fifty yards away, he watched a slender man in a stocking cap plunge a knife into

Kitty's back. Fink remembered that the knife's blade was shiny. "I thought about going downstairs to get my baseball bat," he said.

"Why didn't you?" Cacciatore asked.

Fink shrugged. He went downstairs all right, to a room equipped with a cot, a lamp, and a telephone, but rather than grab his Louisville Slugger or even pick up the phone, he went to sleep. He'd had a long day. Why get into trouble across the street?

"The least he could have done was open the front door to the apartment building, yell out, 'The police are coming!' and lock the door again," Skoller recalled. "This would have protected him from danger and might have stopped the attacker. It made me sick to my stomach dealing with this man." After crossing his name off their list of potential witnesses, Cacciatore and Skoller told Fink a white lie. "We gave him a subpoena and told him to be ready to testify. It was our woefully inadequate attempt at justice—making Fink sweat about being called. He deserved worse."

The prosecution team turned its attention to the other "sickening" witness.

Karl Ross had been drinking most of that night. At about 3:30 a.m. he was sitting in his second-floor apartment in the Tudor building when he heard a noise outside. A woman's voice. Was it someone he knew? Calling for help? The cries came from below his window, the window facing Austin Street. Skittish by nature, the groggy Ross wasn't eager to find out what was happening. He stayed where he was. He waited, hoping the noises would stop. Soon they died down. He relaxed.

A few minutes later another noise startled him. This one came from the back of the building, the side facing the train tracks. Was he surrounded? He heard a scuffling. A muffled cry. The sounds went on and on. Ross stood by his door but didn't open it. He paced behind it, wondering what he should do. At last his curiosity got the better of him. He opened the door a crack.

His door opened on a staircase that led to a narrow vestibule. Ross saw shapes at the foot of the stairs. Bodies. One was Kitty Genovese, lying flat on her back. There was a man with a knife on top of her. Kitty was trying to speak. The man was stabbing her. Then he stopped.

Then the man looked up at Karl Ross.

12

Confessions

At first, Karl Ross told detectives that he had heard screams from the front of the building, the site of the first attack. Later he changed his story. Now that he was thinking straight, he said, he was sure he had heard nothing before the noises from the other direction, outside the door to his apartment, in the stairwell.

The police and prosecutors were willing to bet he was lying. Ross's Austin Street window was almost directly over the spot where Moseley first caught up with Kitty. No neighbor had been closer. Kitty's screams on the sidewalk—*"Oh God he stabbed me! Help me!"*—had been loud enough to wake twelve-year-old Mike Farrar in his bedroom, twenty or more yards farther away in the same building. Her cries woke people five and six floors up in the apartment building across Austin Street and in the West Virginia Apartments farther away. So when Ross flip-flopped and claimed that the first screams he had heard came from the stairwell beyond his door on the opposite side of the building, the cops knew better. While Kitty's initial cries for help had been loud, there were no full-throated screams during the later attack in the stairwell downstairs from Ross's door. By the time Moseley renewed his assault in the stairwell, her punctured lungs could barely fill with air. She was running out of breath.

Ross not only insisted that the only cries he'd heard came from the stairwell: he also denied seeing anyone stabbing her. "We knew he was lying," prosecutor Skoller recalled. They knew because Ross had phoned a friend before calling the police. Sounding frightened, he had said somebody was attacking Kitty Genovese on the stairs.

If he hadn't seen anyone attacking her, how did he know it was Kitty? Pressed on that point, Ross backtracked. He admitted opening his door a crack. "I opened the door enough to listen," he said.

Moseley had a different view. "I was lying between her legs," the cooperative defendant said, "and I heard the door open at the top of the stairs. Out of the corner of my eye I saw a man peeking out at us." In Moseley's account the man at the top of the stairs "shut the door real quick" only to peek out again a moment later.

Finally Ross admitted changing his story. The truth was, he had heard and seen more than he wanted to admit. He'd been drunk and scared, he admitted. Scared of the attacker, who might turn his knife on him, and scared of the police, who would ask who he was, how he knew what he knew, why he sounded drunk. So he had phoned a friend, who told him not to stick his nose in other people's business. Later he phoned his neighbor Carol Tarantino. "I should call the police!" Ross wailed. But he didn't want the cops knocking on his door.

"Come over here. You can call from here," Tarantino said.

At that point the drunken dog-groomer faced another dilemma. Taking the stairs might put him face-to-face with the knife-wielding attacker. Unwilling to open the door, Ross climbed out a window to the building's shingled roof. He clambered to Tarantino's window and tumbled into her apartment. Tarantino then phoned another neighbor, Greta Schwartz, who phoned the Farrars, Kitty and Mary Ann's across-the-hall neighbors. Sophie Farrar shouted, "Call the police!" Finally, at 3:55, Ross phoned the police.

Later, under questioning, Ross explained his thinking that night. He said, "I didn't want to get involved!"

His quote became notorious. Within weeks Ross's line became the unofficial motto of urban apathy. Fittingly enough, nobody remembered who said it.

"It was impossible to decide who was more despicable, Fink or Ross," recalled Skoller. The prosecutors had hoped to put Ross on the witness stand, but decided "that route wasn't available to us. Ross, a man who would do anything to avoid accepting responsibility, might foul up our prosecution with his fabrications." So they sent him home. Ross promptly took a bottle of vodka to Mary Ann's apartment and took a seat as if nothing had happened.

"I sat there drinking with him," Mary Ann says. "I didn't know that he could have saved her. What if he'd opened his door? What if he'd shouted?" Fifty years later she shakes her head. "This man who was afraid of everything . . . he was the last person who should have been behind that door."

Once she learned of the role he had played that night, Mary Ann told Ross to get lost. He took her advice, but his excuse lingered. "I didn't want to get involved" entered the national conversation with a boost from *Life*'s Loudon Wainwright, whose April 10 column, THE DYING GIRL THAT NO ONE HELPED, shared Rosenthal's perspective. Wainwright (father of folksinger Loudon Wainwright III, grandfather of

singer Rufus Wainwright) portrayed Kitty as dying in full view of
more than three-dozen neighbors who watched like a crowd in an
auditorium. In his column the number of witnesses the *Times*' Gansberg got from Commissioner Murphy returns as exactly "thirty-eight
heedless witnesses." Wainwright was careful to credit his source:
"Kitty Genovese, a decent, pretty young woman, was stalked and
stabbed by a man who had followed her home and who took almost
half an hour to kill her. During that bloody little eternity, according
to an extraordinary account published in the *New York Times*, Kitty
screamed and cried repeatedly for help." The neighbors heard her
screams, he wrote, and "understood her cry for help. For the most
part the witnesses, crouching in darkened windows like watchers of
a Late Show, looked on until the play had passed beyond their view.
Then they went back to bed." The columnist quoted Lieutenant Bernard Jacobs of the 102nd Precinct, who reported that multiple witnesses had told police they didn't want to get involved. Wainwright
described the lieutenant waving an arm, saying, "It's a nice neighborhood, isn't it? Doesn't look like a jungle." No one could mistake his
meaning: the people of Kew Gardens had acted like animals.

Lieutenant Jacobs was hardly the first to compare the modern
city to a jungle, but his words hit a nerve. *Izvestia*, the Soviet Union's
daily broadsheet, crowed that the case demonstrated America's "jungle morals." Psychologists joined reporters and pundits in mulling a
story that fed readers' growing uneasiness about the loneliness of
urban life. At a time when young people were moving from their
hometowns to cities, where life was more exciting and more dangerous, a time when young women were beginning to assert their inde-
pendence (or at least reading *The Feminine Mystique* and Helen Gurley
Brown's *Sex and the Single Girl*), a time of Black Power, "Better dead
than red," and not trusting anyone over thirty, when the fabric of
society seemed to fray a little more every day, the killing of Kitty

Genovese tapped wells of feeling in millions, young and old. It filled them with pity and terror.

Lieutenant Jacobs told Wainwright that Kitty would be alive if a single witness had cared enough to pick up the telephone. "All we want is a phone call," he said.

Life magazine readers were incensed. One wrote a letter that typified America's view of Kitty's neighbors:

Sirs:

After reading with disgust your account of the murder of Catherine Genovese and the more than 38 cowards who watched her die, I find it lamentable that these residential barbarians could not be tried as accessories. Then they would be involved.

The phrase "more than 38" suggests how quickly a number can take on a life of its own. The three to four dozen Kew Gardeners the police considered either earwitnesses or eyewitnesses during the first stage of their investigation had somehow become thirty-eight (or even "more than thirty-eight"), a figure the *Times*, *Life*, and other sources accepted as gospel. The number might grow as the story grew, but it would never shrink.

My research for this book led to the detectives' reports of their initial interviews with Kitty's neighbors. A four-page document dated March 20, 1964, presented the detectives' findings to the Queens County District Attorney's Investigation Bureau a week after the crime. The document lists 49 witnesses who saw or heard something on the night Kitty died. Sixteen were eyewitnesses. Many of the witnesses' names were never made public. It is worth noting that the detectives' report on them did not include Sophie Farrar, her hus-

Kitty Genovese tended bar and managed Ev's 11th Hour in Hollis, Queens. (Getty Images)

The Genoveses and three other families lived at 29 St. John's Place in Brooklyn.

The Church of St. Augustine
loomed over their neighborhood in Park Slope.
(Lily Cook)

Kitty received her First
Holy Communion at
St. Augustine's in 1944.
(Lily Cook)

Brooklyn-born Kitty didn't want to leave the city for the suburbs.
(Courtesy of Joe Corrado)

At Prospect Heights High School, the girl identified as "Class Cut-Up" Kitty (lower left) struck a serious pose. (1953 Prospect Heights *Cardinal*)

She flashed a smile for the yearbook.
(1953 Prospect Heights *Cardinal*)

Kitty's 1953
senior photo.
(1953 Prospect
Heights *Cardinal*)

For all cheese cake lovers, here is a product manufactured especially for you by ELAINE VERRELLI and MARY ROBSON The cheese taken out of F, F, & F pizza pies goes into their delicious pastries. So for a pie to end all pies, buy V & R's Charming Cheese Cake at all leading butcher shops and supermarkets. And now, back to the show

We take you to the steps of City Hall where Police Inspector EVELYN FANTI is about to present citations to patrolmen KITTY GENOVESE and PHYLISS TRIMBOLI for their many faithful years of service and for helping our fair city crack down on crime. I see that the inspector is about to begin her speech. Come in, City Hall.—

"Unaccustomed as I am to public speaking, this momentous occasion does call for a few choice words——

A lighthearted class prophecy saw police work in Kitty's future.
(1953 Prospect Heights *Cardinal*)

New Yorkers awaited the opening of the 1964 World's Fair, just north of Kew Gardens.
(Everett Collection)

Sophie Farrar, Kitty's friend and across-the-hall neighbor, in 1963.
(Courtesy of Sophia and Michael Farrar)

The Austin Street sidewalk, scene of the initial attack. (The New York Times/Redux)

Kitty came around the corner where the car is visible, and fell through the door marked by the doormat nearest the car. Her own door is at the lower right. (Eddie Hausner/The New York Times/Redux)

Joseph Fink watched from the lobby of the Mowbray building.

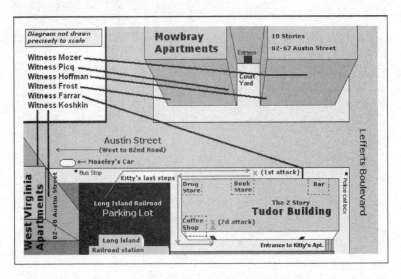

Kew Gardens' Joseph De May prepared a detailed diagram of the crime scene. (Oldkewgardens.com)

Kitty sought refuge at the foot of the stairs to Karl Ross's apartment.

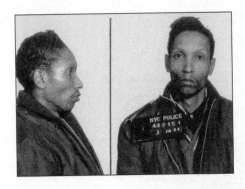

Arrested for a burglary, Winston Moseley soon confessed to murder. (Courtesy of Janine Abel)

Suspect Moseley in a full-body mug shot, never published before. (Courtesy of Janine Abel)

Times reporter Martin Gansberg wrote the front-page story that made news around the world. (Courtesy of Judith Gansberg)

A courtroom
sketch of
Sparrow
in action.
(Courtesy of
Robert Sparrow)

Defense lawyer
Sidney Sparrow
hoped to save
Moseley from the
electric chair.
(Courtesy of
Robert Sparrow)

(BF2) Buffalo, N.Y., March 21--IT'S OVER--Winston Moseley, convicted killer who escaped from a prison guard Monday, stands with FBI special agent Neil J. Welch after he surrendered today to Welch at nearby Grand Island. Moseley gave up after holding a woman and her infant daughter hostage for two hours. (AP Wirephoto) (mrp51725c-e) 1968

Still wearing a hostage's clothes, Moseley surrendered to FBI agent Neil Welch after his 1968 escape.

Fordham professor Harold Takooshian found something "holy" in the Genovese story. (Courtesy of Harold Takooshian)

In 2004 Abraham Rosenthal made a surprise appearance at a Fordham conference on the Genovese case. (Courtesy of Harold Takooshian)

The crime scene in 2013.

Mary Ann Zielonko today.
(Courtesy of Mary Ann Zielonko)

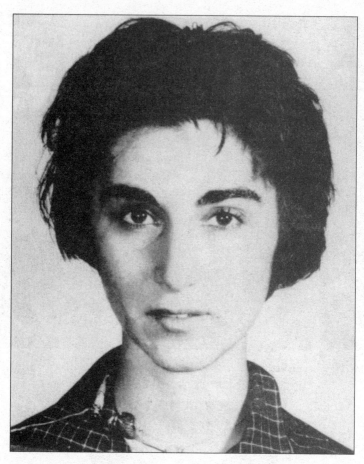

The best-known photo of Kitty Genovese is her 1961 mug shot, taken after a minor gambling arrest. (The New York Times/Redux)

band Joe, and their son Michael, who all heard Kitty's cries during Moseley's first attack but saw nothing when they went to their window. The detectives' list did not include Joseph Fink. It did not include Karl Ross. It was a roundup of interviews with many of Kitty's neighbors, not a definitive accounting of anything.

The Investigation Bureau report featured thirty-eight entries. Some entries noted a detective's interview with two or three witnesses. In all likelihood, someone in the police department counted the entries and passed the total on to Commissioner Murphy, who passed it on to Rosenthal. An innocent mistake, possibly made in a hurry. A clerical error. This is the source of the number that has loomed over Kitty's lonely death.

Thirty-eight. A number so definitive that it would help define the story for fifty years, and so arbitrary that Murphy may as well have picked it out of his hat.

Almost as definitive was another figure Lieutenant Jacobs gave columnist Wainwright: zero. According to Jacobs, that was the number of witnesses who called the police while Kitty was being attacked.

Where did that zero come from? Was the lieutenant simply endorsing the police department's view of the Genovese murder? Had he seen the phone logs, which were never made public? Was he feeding the media false information?

Did he know that the real number wasn't zero?

With help from Lieutenant Jacobs, *Life*'s Wainwright, Mike Wallace of CBS, the *Times*' Rosenthal and Gansberg, and many more, Chief Murphy's version of the Genovese case carried the day. The story that the chief told Rosenthal "beats everything" overshadowed the soon-forgotten double confession in the Barbara Kralik case while police, prosecutors, the press, and the public focused on Kitty Genovese.

. . .

To Mary Ann's surprise, the world went on.

The World's Fair opened on schedule in April, thanks in part to three hundred of Murphy's policemen, backed by twenty-five hundred uniformed Pinkerton cops hired by Robert Moses to keep order at the greatest show in history. Civil-rights activists charged Moses and other fair organizers with unfair hiring practices. They had a point. From construction crews to technical and professional positions, the fair's army of employees was almost 100 percent white. Isaiah Brunson, head of the Brooklyn chapter of CORE, the Congress of Racial Equality, hoped to shut down the fair by having his supporters abandon two thousand cars on streets leading to the fairgrounds. Calling his protest a "stall-in," Brunson threatened Moses with "the biggest traffic jam New York ever had." His activists also picketed outside the fairgrounds and staged a sit-in at the Schaefer Beer pavilion on opening day.

Andrew Goodman was one of the picketers. A Queens College friend of folkie Paul Simon, the twenty-year-old Goodman joined protesters the *Times* described as "bearded and untidy, the seats of their pants muddied from sitting on the soggy ground," a wild-looking bunch that "repelled and fascinated fairgoers." A fresh-faced idealist with sleepy, downturned eyes, Goodman would go from the fair to Meridian, Mississippi, to help register black voters as part of CORE's "Freedom Summer" project. In June he and his CORE colleagues James Chaney and Mickey Schwerner would be abducted by Ku Klux Klansmen, shot dead one by one, and secretly buried just off Mississippi Highway 21.

CORE's World's Fair protest fizzled when traffic flowed smoothly and club-swinging Pinkertons busted up the picket line. Moses held a press conference, squinting under TV lights while he listed some of his fair's many firsts: a total cost of $1 billion; 5,300 newly planted trees; 110 restaurants; eight fountains; and 1,400 new "touch-tone" telephones. There was also the world's largest block of cheese, plus new consumer products including the Ford Mustang, the IBM Selectric typewriter, wheeled toys called "skate-boards," Sony's first video-cassette recorder (weighing 145 pounds), Maxim freeze-dried coffee, Diet Pepsi, and Kellogg's Pop-Tarts. After months of civic hand-wringing, the fair was a qualified hit. If not quite a sensation to rival Beatlemania, it set a record by drawing a million visitors in its first week. "A smasheroo of a world's fair," *Life* called it. Few questioned such oddities as the roster of immortals in its International Wax Museum, which held life-size figures of Superman, Jesus, Cleopatra, the Beatles, and Robert Moses, though pop-art fans looking for Andy Warhol's contribution to the fair went away disappointed.

Under Moses's direction, architect Philip Johnson had asked Warhol, Roy Lichtenstein, Robert Rauschenberg, and other modern artists to create original works for the New York State pavilion. Warhol's fans were eager to see what Andy might add to what promised to be the most Philistine show on earth. He delivered thirteen giant silkscreen mug shots of the FBI's most-wanted fugitives. Governor Nelson Rockefeller, a trustee of the Museum of Modern Art, hated them. Too negative! And too ethnic, since most of the killers and bank robbers in Warhol's baker's dozen were Mafiosi with recognizably Italian names. Moses agreed with Rockefeller. He dispatched a team of construction workers to paint over Warhol's mug shots on the eve of the fair.

Warhol offered to come up with something else. Overnight he produced a giant mug shot of Robert Moses, who was not amused. Philip Johnson said, Thanks, but no thanks, and visitors to the New York pavilion had to settle for Lichtenstein, Rauschenberg, figure skater Dick Button's "Ice-Travaganza" with 150 skaters and one skating chimp, and exhibits including a scale model of the twin skyscrapers planned for the future World Trade Center in lower Manhattan.

"Outside the fairgrounds, cracks in the nation's foundations were becoming too large to ignore," wrote World's Fair chronicler Lawrence Samuel. "Camelot had come and passed." For those who spun through Moses's eighty-nine state-of-the-art turnstiles, however, all was clean efficiency on the 646 landscaped acres *Newsweek* dubbed "the world's biggest playground."

Mary Ann, hoping to forget her troubles for a day, attended the fair with her mother. Caroline Kennedy did the same. On the last day of April, Caroline, who had turned six years old the previous November, reached up to clutch her mother's white-gloved hand. Both wore white coats against an early-spring chill. A few fairgoers wept at the sight of them. Jacqueline Kennedy, determined to make a light-hearted day of it, steered Caroline past the Hall of Presidents with its empty rocking chair. Mother and daughter gaped at the foot-long incisors of the *T. rex* at Dinoland. They patted an animatronic dog in the General Electric pavilion. ("I want to take him home," Caroline said.) The former First Lady examined her hair in different colors at the Clairol exhibit, laughing at the sight of herself as a blonde. She and Caroline got splashed by leaping dolphins at Florida's pavilion and re-splashed on the log-flume ride at Lake Amusement. Climbing into a limousine later, Caroline said, "When are we coming back?"

The Kennedys' limousine departed along the same route from Forest Hills that Indira Gandhi's had taken on the day she broke ground for the fair. Their long black car took the former First Lady and daughter Caroline past Kew Gardens and its L.I.R.R. station, within sight of the Mowbray Apartments, the Tudor building, and the local Catholic church, Our Lady of the Cenacle, where Monsignor Francis Dillon heard several anguished confessions in the weeks after the Genovese murder. A few of Monsignor Dillon's parishioners sought absolution for a sin of omission. They may have told police and reporters that they had no idea what was happening that night, but in the privacy of the confessional they said they felt guilty—they'd done nothing to help that poor girl who got stabbed on the sidewalk.

13

Pleas

The State of New York put Winston Moseley on trial for his life on June 8, 1964, a sunny Monday. By nine that morning reporters and curiosity seekers crowded the steps of the Queens Criminal Courthouse, a white stone box six hundred yards from the spot where Kitty died. The Genovese case had become a story that galvanized gossip rags as well as *Life* and the *Times*. The facts weren't all out yet, but they were sure to tantalize highbrow and lowbrow news outlets, partly due to the "apathy issue," partly due to the age-old specter of black-on-white rape lurking behind the grim facts of Kitty's ordeal.

At 9:15, assistant district attorneys Frank Cacciatore and Charles Skoller pushed a shopping cart full of file folders through the courthouse lobby. One distended folder held the knife Moseley had used on Kitty. The prosecutors bumped their way through the crowd while a loudspeaker in the lobby warned that only a few visitors would be allowed into Judge J. Irwin Shapiro's courtroom. "It was bedlam," Skoller recalled in his memoir. As he and his boss wheeled their files into the small courtroom, "I scanned the spectators' seats, hoping against hope to find someone in Kitty's immediate family present." The sight of Kitty's grieving parents and siblings might harden a jury's hearts against anything Moseley's lawyer would say in his defense. "But it wasn't to be . . . we had learned not to anticipate any cooperation from Kitty's immediate family, her parents or her three brothers and sister." Three months after Kitty's murder, her siblings were still shielding their mother from any details of the crime. As Kitty's brother Vincent told the *Daily News*, "My mother could not handle it. We completely retreated. We dropped off the face of the earth."

Reporters and spectators jostled for seats as Judge Shapiro, a stickler for punctuality, banged his gavel to its sounding block at 9:30.

Shapiro, fifty-nine, ruled his redwood-paneled courtroom in a style that matched his upright posture. With silver-gray hair and a classic profile, the judge reminded spectators of actor Charlton Heston. Brilliant and prickly, he was known to show unprepared lawyers his displeasure by spinning around in his chair, letting them make their cases to the back of his head. Shapiro was also an avowed opponent of the death penalty, and as he nodded to the prosecution and defense attorneys on this bright spring morning he was presiding over a trial that almost everyone expected to end with a sentence of death. No other result would satisfy a public that Bob Sparrow, the defense lawyer's son, recalls as "avid, if not bloodthirsty."

The People of the State of New York against Winston Moseley commenced with Assistant District Attorney Cacciatore's opening statement. Cacciatore began by standing in front of the jury box looking each juror straight in the eye: eleven men and one woman—eight white and four black—each one getting the personal treatment from the folksy little assistant DA, who only stood five foot five.

"The People will show," he said, "that after three a.m. on March thirteenth, screams were heard by many people. 'Help me, help me, I'm being stabbed!' Several witnesses will testify that they looked onto Austin Street and saw a man attacking a girl, or a woman; that one of them opened his window and yelled out 'Leave that girl alone!'" While Cacciatore began a detailed description of Moseley's attack, the accused sat at the defense table beside his court-appointed lawyer, Sidney Sparrow. Freshly barbered and shaved, dressed in black pants and a black sport coat over an orange plaid shirt, Moseley looked sleepy, like a student sitting through a lecture that bored him. But the jurors weren't bored.

"Frank's opening was having the effect on the jurors that we were hoping for," Cacciatore's colleague Skoller recalled. "With each new brutal detail, they seemed to shift their eyes from Frank and glared at Moseley." The prosecutors had decided not to mention the neighbors' failure to help Kitty, "so the jurors wouldn't shift their fury from Moseley to Kitty's neighbors." To focus the jurors' fury on the defendant, Cacciatore spent ten minutes describing Moseley's assault in terms so graphic that the newspapers couldn't report them. "I hope you will understand. I am calling a spade a spade," he said. The courtroom was quiet. "The People will prove that he deliberately, with malice aforethought, killed Kitty Genovese. The People will prove each and every element to be a responsible, a deliberate, a willful, a coordinated act, and the People will expect at the appropriate time that you will bring in the verdict which is justified." His meaning was clear: a verdict of guilty, a sentence of death.

After a paper-shuffling pause Sidney Sparrow rose to face the jury. Taller and more snappily dressed than the rumpled, balding Cacciatore, his diction more precise, Sparrow opened by admitting that his client was a killer. Gesturing toward Moseley, he called the defendant a victim of his upbringing, "a pawn between his mother and father." An innocent child corrupted by faithless Fannie and jealous Alphonso, Winston was "a very intelligent, shy, quiet and retiring youngster" puzzled by the story his mother told about a cancer in her belly, a boy fixated on women's abdomens, "initiated into the concepts of sex by a Negress . . . a married woman, too, just as his mother had been." Another unfaithful wife. "And Winston Moseley began to more and more brood," Sparrow told the jury, "and his mind, without his knowing it, was changing." Here was the core of Sparrow's plan to save his client from the electric chair: the idea that a maddening life had turned Moseley into a killer. A killer, but not technically a murderer.

"Winston came to feel that one of the things wrong with the world was prejudice against the Negro," Sparrow continued. Moseley's boss might let him drive the boss's daughter home, but the man would never see Winston as an equal. So he seethed. "He was intelligent, and felt he could have gone much, much further had he not been a Negro." During the winter of 1963–'64, Sparrow claimed, the seeds of Moseley's madness bloomed into a poisonous hatred of women.

Except for his wife. Betty Moseley, Sparrow said, was Winston's "perfect wife." Sparrow told the court that Moseley had wanted to be a good husband to Betty. Lowering his voice, he told the jury that Moseley had tried and tried to have a normal sex life with Betty, sometimes overcoming his impotence "by an act of sodomy— cunnilingus, as it's known in medicine."

Next, Sparrow segued from sex to murder. On the night of February 28, 1964, he said, Moseley had gone for a late-night drive. He came across a young Negro woman parking her car in Ozone Park, a few blocks from his own house. Sparrow recounted how Moseley shot Annie Mae Johnson while she pleaded for her life, how he tried to have sex with her body and then, in his impotent rage, set fire to her house and her genitals. And then he spent a pleasant weekend with Betty and the kids. Did that sound like what a sane man would do? Now Sparrow moved forward two weeks from the Johnson murder to March 13, 1964. "Kitty Genovese, whom he never knew, meant nothing to him except that she was another symbol of womanhood." He promised to call psychiatrists who would testify that his client was psychotic, a term popularized by Alfred Hitchcock's 1960 movie *Psycho.* More than that, Moseley was a sort of psycho who might have disgusted even Hitchcock's twisted Norman Bates. "A necrophiliac," Sparrow said, enunciating each syllable. "An individual prone to vent his spleen and his sex upon dead bodies." Owing to his troubled boyhood and sexual confusion, Sparrow said, Winston's fixation on women's stomachs and their blood "finally erupted into this horrible series of atrocities."

Sparrow held up his hands as if to say, *Does that sound like a sane man?* Now it was his turn to look the jurors in the eye. "You promised me, each of you, and swore on your oath that you will apply the law," he said. "And if by reason of insanity Winston Moseley is exculpated from responsibility, it is your obligation to bring a verdict of 'not guilty by reason of insanity.'"

Judge Shapiro announced a recess until the following day. "Defendant is remanded," he said. Betty Moseley watched a pair of guards lead her husband out of the courtroom in shackles.

The uproar over Kitty's murder brought demands to reform the way distress calls reached the police. Boston, Chicago, Phila-

delphia, San Francisco, and other cities employed central switch-
boards to handle emergency calls, but New York still used a feeder
system. New Yorkers could dial "0" or try the police number on the
cover of their phone books—a different number for every borough.
(In Queens it was JA6-1700, the *JA* standing for "Jamaica.") Either
way the call would be routed to the borough's police communications desk, where a duty officer asked for the caller's name and
address as well as a description of the emergency, then relayed details
to the nearest precinct house. Citizens could also phone their local
precinct houses themselves. In that case a telephone switchboard
(TS) officer could dispatch a squad car, switch the call to the borough's communications desk, or ignore it as a prank or false alarm.
Most calls were recorded in a TS log, but not all of them, and delays
could occur at each decision point. Police responded to some emer-
gencies in minutes, while frantic callers a few blocks away might wait
for hours or get no response at all.

In a *Times* follow-up to his now-famous story on Kitty's murder,
Martin Gansberg reported that the NYPD was working on "a single
police telephone number for all five boroughs to speed emergency
calls." The department considered using numbers corresponding to
words: FOR HELP, POLICE, or 2-6-7, which spelled *COP*. "However, a
spokesman for the New York Telephone Company said the use of a
word was being discounted because some people would have trouble
with the spelling, no matter how simple the word." Commissioner
Murphy announced that his department was eager to speed responses
to emergency calls. "I would like to emphasize that the identity of
witnesses remains confidential," he said, but it wasn't always so: many
TS officers still asked callers to identify themselves. The commissioner urged reporters to help fight crime by encouraging their readers to phone the police. "He cited an article in *The New York Times*
about the slaying of Miss Catherine Genovese as an illustration of

'the kind of thing that alerts the public,'" modest Gansberg reported, neglecting to mention that he had written the article or that Murphy had tipped the *Times* to the story in the first place.

Gansberg also left out a factor that often thwarted emergency response: some citizens disliked the police. Many Americans—New Yorkers in particular, perhaps—viewed policemen (the NYPD was more than 99 percent male) as bullies with guns. Kitty, Mary Ann, and their lesbian friends certainly saw Commissioner Murphy's 17,658 patrol officers and 3,277 detectives that way, but you didn't have to be gay to mistrust the cops. "Have you ever reported anything to the police?" a *Times* reader asked in a letter to the editor. "If you did, you would know that you are subjected to insults and abuse from annoyed police such as 'Why don't you move out of the area?' or 'Why bother us?' Or you will have a call answered forty-five minutes after it was put in." According to another letter-writer, "Nothing annoys a precinct desk captain more than a call after ten o'clock." Another wrote, "I heard screaming on the street several times, called the police and was politely told to mind my own business." Some Kew Gardens residents would cross the street to avoid crossing paths with the local beat cop. "In those days the police were not your friend," one says, "and you certainly didn't call the cops if you could help it. You didn't want to deal with *them*. You call, you got quizzed. They want your name. Where you live, why you're calling . . . and all this time nothing is happening. Sometimes the apathetic one was wearing a badge."

On Tuesday, the second day of the trial, Cacciatore called Robert Mozer to the stand. Mozer lived on the seventh floor of the Mowbray Apartments, the building that loomed over the crime scene on the north side of Austin Street. Kitty's cries woke him from a sound sleep between 3:15 and 3:20 a.m. "I heard a girl saying, 'Help me, help me.'" Mozer told the court. He said he went to his window and saw a man bent over a woman on the sidewalk, striking her. A domestic spat, he figured—unpleasant but not unusual outside Bailey's Pub. Still it wasn't right to hit a woman. Mozer lifted his window and yelled, "Leave that girl alone!" The attacker ran away. Mozer watched Kitty stand up and walk to the corner drugstore toward the railroad tracks. Then she wandered around the corner, out of sight. He went back to bed.

Stewardess Andrée Picq lived on the Mowbray's fourth floor, three floors below Mozer. She testified that she heard Mozer shout, "Leave that girl alone!" and saw the attacker skitter away. Unlike Mozer, Picq stayed at her window, "kind of frozen," she recalled. "A few minutes later the man came back." She watched the man, now wearing a sporty fedora with a feather in the brim, check the doors at the train station. Finding them locked, he walked toward the back of the Tudor building. Then she lost sight of him. She dialed the police, "but I was gasping for breath," she testified. Unsure of her English, unsure of what she had just seen, afraid to identify herself to the authorities, she put down the phone.

"Anything else you saw, Miss Picq?" Cacciatore asked.

"No," she said. After the man rounded the corner of Kitty's building, "I did not see anything. But I heard the last two screams. 'Help, help.'"

Another witness, Irene Frost, testified that she saw Kitty kneeling on the sidewalk and heard her call out, "Please help me, God. I have been stabbed."

Later that morning Cacciatore called Sophie Farrar to the stand. Sophie, the neighbor who invited Kitty over for coffee, the one Kitty confided in, hated thinking that her friend would never have the chance to explore her options in life. She wondered whether Kitty would have stayed with Mary Ann or gotten her operation and had children someday or—who could say in the 1960s and beyond?—done both? Nobody would ever know. Winston Moseley had stolen Kitty's future. Now four-foot-eleven Sophie, barely visible to the gallery as she stepped past the defense table, glanced at Moseley. If a look could kill there would have been no need for an electric chair. Moments later she was telling the court about hearing Kitty's voice during Moseley's initial attack. "I heard a scream. Then I listened and didn't hear anything. I went back to bed." Half an hour passed before the phone rang. Greta Schwartz, another neighbor, said someone was stabbing Kitty Genovese.

"What? Where?" Sophie asked.

"In the hall—downstairs from Karl's apartment!" Schwartz said.

"Call the police!"

Sophie Farrar was the last eyewitness to testify. Cacciatore didn't want the others, particularly Fink and Ross, to give the defense a chance to point an accusing finger at Kitty's neighbors the way the *Times*, *Life*, and so many others had done. To Frank Cacciatore, the only monster in Shapiro's courtroom was sitting at the defense table, and it was Cacciatore's job to make sure that he got the two thousand volts he deserved.

After Sophie stepped down, Cacciatore introduced the state's next witness: "Miss Zielonko." Mary Ann had met with the attorneys before the trial—meetings she barely remembers today. "I'd been drinking day and night," she says. She agreed to go along with the fiction that she was nothing more than Kitty's friend and roommate, a lie that suited both sides. The prosecution wanted to keep the spotlight on Moseley's cruelty, while the defense hoped jurors would believe that Moseley was insane. Kitty's sexuality would be a distraction either way. It stayed secret.

Witness Zielonko made a lasting impression on the men in the courtroom. "One could not help staring admiringly at Mary Ann as she took the stand," Skoller recalled. "With her short blonde hair, she was stunningly beautiful, bearing a remarkable resemblance to Hollywood icon Kim Novak." According to Skoller's widow, "Charlie was quite taken by Mary Ann. As for her being a lesbian, he wanted to keep that quiet, partly to protect Kitty's family and partly because it could tar Kitty's reputation."

Mary Ann identified the brown billfold she had given Kitty for Christmas, which was duly labeled People's Exhibit 9. Then Cacciatore held up an item recovered from the crime scene.

"Those are Kitty's house keys and car keys," she said.

"Where did you last see them?"

"On the floor." Mary Ann was whispering now. She had seen the keys in the bloodstained vestibule after the ambulance took Kitty away.

The judge scolded her. "I can't hear you, Miss. If you want to talk to yourself, you might as well get off the witness stand. The jury wants to hear you. Keep your voice up."

"I think I saw them on the floor," she said.

After another minute, the public performance Mary Ann had dreaded was over. She was free to go. On her way out, she passed within a few feet of Winston Moseley. She had imagined staring him down, spitting at him, slapping him. She had even imagined killing him, a fantasy that disintegrated now that the killer was sitting in front of her. She couldn't bring herself to look at him. She left the courtroom, ignoring the reporters in the press gallery and the lobby. Mary Ann walked down the courthouse steps, left Queens, and never looked back. She never set foot in Kew Gardens again.

Later on the trial's second day, Detective John Carroll recounted the initial police response to the crime, the subsequent investigation, Moseley's arrest and confession. Cacciatore then called Kitty's uncle Vito Genovese—no relation to the mobster, who had spent the past five years in Atlanta Federal Penitentiary—to confirm the official identification of his niece's body in the morgue at Queens General Hospital. Next Dr. William Benenson, the city's assistant medical examiner, described Kitty's autopsy. ("There was no way I could stay to hear that," Mary Ann says.) Benenson listed fourteen wounds including "two stab wounds that penetrated the right and left chest, releasing air into the chest cavity. As a result, the lungs were compressed, breathing became impossible, and she died."

Lieutenant Bernard Jacobs, the detective who had compared Kew Gardens to a jungle, told the court how he had dispatched two policemen to search the weeds by the parking lot at Raygram, the defendant's workplace, where they found Kitty's billfold. Jacobs had sent Detective Mitch Sang to Moseley's home, where Sang found a serrated, bone-handled hunting knife in a toolbox, where Moseley told him it would be, the knife now labeled People's Exhibit 12. Jacobs admitted being impressed by the accused. "His speech was excellent," the lieutenant told the court, with "a well-modulated voice and carefully chosen words. I was quite taken with it." He told of an instance when Moseley seemed to have a pang of something like regret. It was after Moseley signed his confession, Jacobs said, just before detectives walked him through the station house lobby, where a bunch of news photographers waited. "He asked me if it was all right if he covered his face," Jacobs testified. "I asked him why. 'Because I have a father,' he said. 'I also have a wife, and this is a pretty shameful thing.'"

Sitting beside his lawyer three months later, Moseley didn't look ashamed. He looked blank, peering past Cacciatore as the assistant district attorney snatched a document from the files he and Skoller had wheeled into court. Moseley's confession was ten pages long. It contained details that the press and public hadn't seen. Reporters leaned forward to hear, but they had nothing to worry about. As he turned to face the jury, Cacciatore's voice filled the courtroom. He proceeded to read the confession in full.

From page two:

I ran after her and stabbed her twice in the back. Somebody yelled and I was frightened, so I jumped back into the car, backed the car to the nearest cross street. . . . I decided that even though this person had yelled, they weren't going to come down to the street to see what happened to her, and I noticed as I was backing the car back that the woman had gotten up and appeared to be going around the corner, so I came back thinking I would find her.

Moseley looked straight ahead as Cacciatore turned a page.

She wasn't in the train station. It was locked, so I said to myself, "Well, perhaps she is in one of these hallways." The second door I tried opened, and there she was laying on the floor. When she saw me she started screaming again, so I stabbed her a few more times. She seemed to quiet down a little bit, she wasn't really struggling that hard with me now, so I lifted up her skirt and I cut off her girdle. I cut or pulled her panties off and she had a sanitary pad and I picked that out and threw it away and I stabbed her again in the stomach. I cut off her brassiere, and I don't remember whether I cut her blouse or not, and I took one of the false pads that she had in the brassiere.

Cacciatore kept reading.

Question: Did she finally stop screaming?
Answer: Yes.

Skoller kept his eyes on the jury. Some jurors looked angry or ill. A minute of this graphic confession seemed to go on much longer. Cacciatore wanted it that way. He pressed on.

I laid on top of her and I attempted to have sexual intercourse with her, but I was unable to, as I was impotent . . . and though I had an orgasm, I was not able to penetrate into her.

When he finished reading, the assistant DA turned to Judge Shapiro. "The People rest, if your Honor pleases." Four hours into the trial's second day, the state had presented its case. As Skoller wrote, "We deliberately kept our case brief, so as not to muddy the waters. We wanted to leave no doubt that Moseley was Kitty's killer, that he was viciously brutal, and that he was in command of his faculties when he committed the crime. We anticipated the insanity defense by repeating Moseley's rational, detailed descriptions."

Shapiro announced a midday recess. With Moseley's confession fresh in their minds, some of the spectators skipped lunch.

In the afternoon Sidney Sparrow took his turn facing the jury. The dapper Sparrow had two goals in mind. He wanted to convince the jurors that his client was human, and that he was crazy. Seeing Winston Moseley as human would make it harder to sentence him to death. Deciding that he was insane would make him innocent of murder.

Fannie Moseley was the first defense witness. At forty-nine, the killer's plump, self-assured mother made herself comfortable on the witness stand. She swore that her son was a good seed gone bad, "a quiet child" corrupted by her husband, "a very erratic person."

Alphonso, she said, had been a bad father despite the fact that he had raised Winston, another man's son, as his own. He had even threatened her life. "I told Winston that Alphonso was following me in his car, threatening to shoot me with a gun," she testified. "This upset him very much, and he spoke to his father about it." Fannie apparently didn't know that her son had offered to shoot her himself if it would keep Alphonso out of trouble. Describing the happy home she shared with Winston and his family, she wept. The house in South Ozone Park was a happy, safe place, she said, thanks to Winston and his prize German shepherd, Wolfie.

"Is Wolfie a gentle dog?" defense attorney Sparrow asked.

"No, a ferocious dog. If anybody comes near, Wolfie would tear him to pieces. She has bitten several people."

"And Winston?"

Fannie smiled. "We all loved Winston," she said. "Winston was just our king."

Alphonso Moseley followed his estranged wife to the witness stand. Gangly, graying Alphonso came burdened with a lengthy rap sheet: more than a dozen arrests for assault, disturbing the peace, and receiving stolen property. At forty-nine he looked older than Fannie, his still-nimble hands as weathered as the skin around his eyes. He settled into the witness chair with a glance toward Winston, who returned his daddy's gaze with a look that may have been love.

Alphonso told the court how the boy he considered his son had been shuttled from Harlem to Michigan and eventually back to New York. He said Winston had always shied from conflict except for the time he attacked the boy who was beating up his daddy, and put the boy's eye out. He said Pauline, Winston's first wife, cheated on him— she was faithless like his mother—but he'd finally settled down with Betty in South Ozone Park, a family man with a steady job.

"Was he happy?" Sparrow asked.

Alphonso thought about that. "I never was able to crash his inner self," he said. "We were pals, but I never could crash his surface. He always had his own way."

Winston's wives came next. Pauline Moseley, still using Winston's surname seven years after he divorced her, recalled meeting him when he was seventeen and she was fifteen. They married two years later, but Pauline grew tired of his long silences and solitary habits. She admitted cheating on her young husband with the bartender who lived downstairs. She recalled the time Winston threatened to shoot her—how she had taken the gun and aimed it at him, only to see him shrug and say, "Kill me." But Pauline wasn't a killer. She put the gun down, and Winston never hurt anyone as far as she knew. He spent his off hours tending his ant farm, feeding the ants bread crumbs and cockroaches.

"Would he give them dead roaches?" Sparrow asked.

"Dead roaches, live roaches. I object," Cacciatore said.

"Overruled." Judge Shapiro allowed Pauline to explain that her husband fed his ants live roaches. The ants climbed on the larger insect and killed it with a thousand bites. Pauline went on to describe the time someone knocked Winston's ant farm onto the floor. "He chased everyone out so we wouldn't step on them. He went around on his knees, picking them up ant by ant, and put them in the cage."

Next, Sparrow called Betty Moseley. Twenty-four-year-old Betty had spent the ten weeks since her husband's arrest looking after Mark, Kerry, the dogs, and the ants, keeping up payments on the house and two cars, avoiding reporters who rang the doorbell and looked in the windows for a peek at the sex killer's family. Dressed in her nurse's uniform, she gathered up her dignity and swore to tell the whole truth. She earned "ninety to ninety-two dollars a week" as a registered nurse, Betty testified. Mr. Zeidman at Raygram had recently given her husband a raise. So no, they weren't hurting for money. Her sex life with Winston was "normal," she said, though he had needed cunnilingus "as a stimulus" lately, as his habits changed. Until the last few months he had been an occasional drinker. Lately he'd been drinking so much that it was a wonder he stayed so thin. Before, Winston had been one of the best-dressed, best-groomed men in the neighborhood, but lately he had let himself go. "I had to tell him to take a bath," she said.

"Did he love you?"

"I felt that he loved me," Betty said.

After she stepped down, Sparrow spent a moment shuffling papers. If there had been Tony awards for defense lawyers, Sidney Sparrow might have been nominated every year. At last Judge Shapiro broke the silence: "Call your next witness."

Sparrow let another second pass. "Winston Moseley," he said.

14

Questions for the Devil

Moseley stood. It was his turn to serve as a witness. He stepped past the prosecution table, his heels clicking on the tile floor. After two days of testimony detailing his crimes, it must have surprised some of the spectators and jury members to see how small the monster was—just five foot eight, 120 pounds.

Moseley put his left hand on the court clerk's Bible, raised his knife hand, and swore to tell nothing but the truth. He sat on the edge of the witness chair and folded his hands in his lap.

Sidney Sparrow began in a conversational tone. "Winston, how old are you?"

"Twenty-nine."

Judge Shapiro interrupted. "Please call the defendant either 'Mr. Defendant' or 'Mr. Moseley.'"

"Very well, sir." Sparrow guided his client through yet another account of his troubled upbringing. Moseley recalled trying to fit in with other children. "But I was not very friendly," he said.

"Did you like other fellows or girls your own age?" Sparrow asked.

"I would almost have to buy friends. If you get children interested in something, they'll stay around, so I used to make small wooden guns."

The lonesome defendant disappointed some of the spectators, but Loudon Wainwright considered Moseley "a very special murderer." To the *Life* columnist, "The most shocking thing about Winston Moseley is the cool delicacy of his face. Framed by a perfectly symmetrical cap of black hair, it is all smooth olive and shadows, and the eyes look out from a distance somehow deeper than their sockets. When Moseley speaks, his mouth works with a dainty economy." Other writers called Moseley catlike, but at the same time there was something insectile about him. His sexual habits might invert those of *Mantis religiosa*, the predator that mates and then kills, but with his wide, watchful eyes and a body that was all angles, he looked like he could sit motionless as a mantis for hours, then spring to the attack.

Moseley admitted stealing TVs and radios that Alphonso resold out of his repair shop in Corona. Then, in January 1964, as he recalled, his late-night excursions took on a different tone. With Betty working the night shift at Elmhurst Hospital, he began staying up late drinking beer, watching TV, and thinking. He was thinking about more than stealing small appliances. He was thinking about sex. He would tuck the boys into bed, then slip out of the house. From January to March "I did maybe four or five rapes," Moseley testified in his even voice. "I had a screwdriver, and it would just be a question of stopping a woman alone early in the morning. I'd take her to an empty lot and tell her to lay down, and they would never resist."

"Did any of them disrobe?" the judge asked.

"One volunteered to take off her clothes, and I was not for that idea."

"Did you at any time attempt to kill anybody?"

"I had gone out with the idea, yes."

"Why?"

"Well, an idea would come into my mind and it would override any other ideas I had, and I would just have to complete that idea."

"What do you mean?"

"It was to me a compulsion."

Prompted by defense lawyer Sparrow, Moseley described stalking and shooting Annie Mae Johnson two weeks before he killed Kitty. After setting fire to her genitals he drove home, washed up, ate breakfast, and went to work. "I always went to work," he said.

Sparrow nodded. Twenty-five years of litigation had made him an expert at reading juries. He thought the jurors were now asking themselves a question, and it was the question he wanted them to ask. Was this a sane man talking?

"Did there come a time on March thirteenth when you again left the house?"

"Yes," Moseley said.

"What did you intend to do that night?"

"Finding a woman and killing her."

"Had you any specific color in mind?"

"Well, I intended to kill a white woman, yes. To see if there might be some difference."

"Tell us what you did, please."

Moseley shifted in the witness chair. "Well, I left the house about one-thirty or two o'clock. It took me until about three to find one that I could catch up with. In a red car. I followed it, and it pulled into a parking lot."

"A white woman."

"Yes, she was."

"Did you make up your mind to kill her?"

"Yes."

In his soft, matter-of-fact voice, Moseley recounted putting on a stocking cap as a disguise. He stepped out of his car. There was a brief chase, he said ("I could run much faster than she could"), before he jumped on Kitty's back and stabbed her twice. The knife went deep. She howled in surprise and terror. Someone shouted from the apartment building across the street: "*Leave that girl alone!*"

"Why didn't you go home?" Sparrow asked.

"I did not think the person who called would come down to help her."

He retreated to his Corvair and backed it into the shadows where no one could read his license plate. He replaced his stocking cap with a fedora that had a feather in the brim, the better to confuse any onlookers, and returned to look for Kitty in the train station's waiting room. Empty. He crossed the L.I.R.R. parking lot and tried a door on the south side of the Tudor building, facing the railroad tracks. "She was in there," Moseley testified. Unable to climb the stairs, Kitty cowered on the floor. "As soon as she saw me, she started screaming, so I stabbed her to stop her from screaming."

Sparrow nodded as if to say, *Of course, who wouldn't?* In private moments he had no trouble admitting that he found his client as loathsome as everyone else did. He had a healthy respect for Moseley's intellect but considered him a particular sort of modern devil, a soul-less psychopath, worse than an animal because he was more dangerous. The creepier he sounded, the better, Sparrow thought, because if Moseley was insane he could be found innocent of murder.

"Tell us what else happened."

Moseley narrated his attacks on Kitty in harrowing detail. At one point he added, "She was having her menstruation period at this time." Sparrow remembered the court-appointed psychologists who noted that three of Moseley's victims were menstruating when he attacked them. He may have been among a small number of serial killers who are drawn to their victims' scent.

Judge Shapiro broke in again. "You wanted to finish the job by killing her?"

"Yes."

"Did you think back about killing Kitty Genovese after doing it? Did you feel sorry for her?"

"No."

"Do you feel sorry for her today?"

"No."

Sparrow felt he had made his case. If Moseley was governed by compulsion, not reason, the jury could find him innocent. Sparrow had one more matter to discuss. "Would you tell us what your feelings were with regards to cleanliness?"

"I like to be clean. I like to be neat," the defendant said. "I do not like my hands to be dirty, no."

"Did you feel that your hands were dirty when they had blood on them?"

"I washed them, yes."

With a little bow to the assistant district attorney, Sparrow said, "Your witness, Mr. Cacciatore."

The prosecutor walked Moseley through his youth again. He asked about the animals on his grandmother's farm. There were cows, horses, pigs, chickens, and ants. "Seeing ants build tunnels and scavenge for food—it was like watching a city, wasn't it?"

"You might compare it to a city," Moseley said.

Cacciatore sounded like he knew about ants. He said, "There would be a queen ant directing the operation."

Moseley corrected him. "There would always be a queen ant, but they don't direct the operation. The queen ant is only to produce more ants. The workers and soldiers take care of the business of the ant colony."

Cacciatore stood corrected. He looked impressed. Moving on through Moseley's work at Raygram and his interest in baseball, he asked, "How about Maris? Today he had a two-base hit." But Moseley wasn't very interested in Roger Maris, Mickey Mantle, or anyone wearing pinstripes other than the rumpled Cacciatore, whom he watched closely, waiting for these questions to segue from baseball to murder. It didn't take long. The assistant DA mentioned cunnilingus again—a topic suggesting deviance if not insanity—before returning to the night Moseley went out for a drive, looking for a white woman.

"Did you know what you were doing? When you were driving, I mean?"

"Yes."

That sounded rational—a point for the state. Moseley testified that he had followed Kitty at a safe distance, observing the speed limit, and parked within striking distance of her. He testified that he had worn work gloves so as not to leave fingerprints. Cacciatore was building a case around the defendant's clear thinking and planning, which were not the same as sanity but might be close enough. He had been delighted when Moseley corrected him about the queen ant's role, sounding as sane as a biology professor. Could such a man be so crazy that he didn't know it was wrong to stab a defenseless woman to death?

He asked about Moseley's tactics. After running Kitty down on the sidewalk and stabbing her in the back, he stabbed her a second time. "You were going to immobilize her, isn't that so?"

"I felt that I would completely kill her," Moseley said.

"Well now, after the second stab, did she go down?"

"Yes."

"And was there yelling?"

"Somebody did yell from a window, yes."

Cacciatore was warming up. "Now you became frightened, huh?"

"Yes. Startled."

"Startled! Frightened for yourself? What did you do?"

"I went back to my car to move it." He parked, changed hats, and returned to the sidewalk, checking doors until he found Kitty. The step-by-step approach of a sensible hunter.

"You saw the girl lying on the floor, isn't that so? And she started to scream."

"Right."

"As she started to scream"—this was the part of the story that had made one of Sidney Sparrow's assistants throw up—"She started to scream, and you stabbed her in the throat. That is where the voice was coming from, isn't that so?"

Moseley said, "That's right."

"So, *logically*, you stabbed her in the throat so she would stop screaming. Does that make sense to you?"

Moseley said it made sense to him at the time. So did removing one of his gloves so that he could pull down his zipper. So did waiting until she quit resisting so much—"when she was laying fairly still and fairly quiet"—before he raped her. So did performing cunnilingus on his helpless victim, because that was what he always did. So did penetrating her with the knife when he couldn't keep his erection, persisting until he completed the sexual part of his assault. "I laid on the girl," he testified, "and I did not have an erection, but I did have an orgasm." After that it made sense to pick Kitty's billfold off the bloodstained floor. Finding forty-nine dollars inside, he stuck the money in his pocket.

"Forty-nine dollars?" Again Cacciatore sounded impressed.

"That's being practical."

"*Practical?*"

"Why would I throw money away?" Moseley asked, reasonably enough.

Cacciatore nodded. Moseley sounded about as rational as a serial sex killer was likely to sound. Now Cacciatore turned up the heat on him. "Isn't it true," he asked, "that Mr. Sparrow told you the only defense you had was to plead insanity?"

Moseley said, "That's true."

"Do you feel that you are insane, really?"

The killer considered the question. "I never really thought I was insane," he replied. "But after listening to your summation of what I have done, it doesn't sound like something an ordinary person would do."

"So you feel that what you did must have been done by some kind of a nut?"

For once the accused raised his voice a notch. "No. I don't say that. I just don't feel that it was something normal, as you call normal."

"As *I* call normal!"

After a flurry of objections, Cacciatore challenged the witness. "Do you have any concept of the truth?" he asked.

Moseley shifted in his seat. "Yes."

"When you stood here and the clerk told you to raise your right hand and swear to tell the truth, what did that mean to you?"

"It meant I should tell you whatever you ask, which I am doing."

"When you raise your hand, do you raise it to God, sir?"

"Objection!" Sparrow shouted.

"Sustained," the judge said.

With a glare at the witness, Cacciatore said, "I have no more questions." Moseley returned to his seat at the defense table, unruffled.

Defense lawyer Sparrow brought him back to the stand for a single question: "Did you kill Barbara Kralik?" Kralik was the third murder victim he'd claimed during his confession binge in the station house, leading to the *Daily News* headline TWO ADMIT SAME SLAYING, which led in turn to the police commissioner's telling editor Rosenthal to focus on the Genovese case.

"Yes," Moseley lied. Sparrow was satisfied—who but a madman confesses to a murder he didn't commit?

"Stand down," the judge told Moseley.

Now the defense called Dr. Oscar Diamond, director of the Manhattan State Mental Hospital on Ward's Island. Diamond's credentials took almost a minute to enumerate: "Diplomate of the American Board of Psychiatry and Neurology, Fellow of the American Psychiatric Association . . ." Judge Shapiro boiled them down for the jury: "He is a high-class psychiatrist, well recognized, a man of standing and authority." Diamond swore that in his expert opinion Winston Moseley had *not* known that killing Kitty Genovese was wrong. "He told me that he felt his mind was deteriorating and he tried desperately to think differently. His emotions were flat."

Another defense witness, Dr. Emil Winkler, chief of psychology at Kings County Hospital, testified that Moseley's knowledge of right and wrong was "severely impaired." On cross-examination, Cacciatore greeted Winkler with a look that Wolfie the watchdog might give a mailman. "You said *impaired*, Doctor, but not destroyed."

"I said *severely* impaired."

"But not destroyed." Waving a finger at the flustered psychiatrist,

Cacciatore asked how a man who tracked his prey from Hollis to Kew Gardens, who moved his car after somebody saw him, who changed hats to disguise his appearance, who then made his escape, discarded evidence, and washed blood off the murder weapon *didn't know that what he was doing was wrong!* Winkler backtracked. He hemmed and hawed. As detective chief Seedman gleefully recalled, Cacciatore "so emotionally pummeled" the unfortunate psychiatrist "that the doctor defecated in his pants on the witness chair."

So ended the defense case. Cacciatore answered the defense psychologists by calling Dr. Frank Cassino, chief psychiatrist at Wyckoff Heights Hospital. Cassino claimed that the defendant did in fact know right from wrong. Admitting that he had never met or spoken to Winston Moseley, he swore that reading others' reports and observing the defendant's behavior during the trial made him certain that Moseley was guilty under the so-called M'Naghten rule that governed such cases. The rule dated back to a British murder trial in 1843, when a lunatic named Daniel M'Naghten shot the prime minister's secretary, mistaking the poor secretary for the prime minister. M'Naghten was acquitted under the novel plea "not guilty by reason of insanity." Other killers had followed his lead for 121 years. The vast majority lost their cases, but a few won acquittal by convincing a judge or jury that they suffered from a "defect of reason" that kept them from understanding the nature of their crimes. To be guilty of doing evil, a defendant had to be in possession of his faculties—had to know the difference between good and evil and *choose* evil.

The insanity defense never made perfect sense. In the Genovese case it led to hairsplitting between the prosecution and defense over issues including "the difference between intellect and conscious knowledge." Judge Shapiro refereed, ordering the lawyers to state their arguments as clearly as possible. His frustration was more than procedural. Like the attorneys, the judge was grappling with a M'Naghtenous question no court was fully equipped to answer: Can a person know the difference between right and wrong and still do wrong? To convict Moseley, the state needed to prove that the answer was yes. Doing that, however, required knowing the exact meanings of *right* and *wrong*, and even *know*. It also called for reading Moseley's mind. Such matters might best be left to philosophers and psychics. The law left Cacciatore needing to convince the jurors that Moseley had weighed good and evil in his head, like Lucifer, and chosen evil, while Sparrow needed to convince them that Moseley couldn't tell the difference.

Cross-examining prosecution psychiatrist Cassino, Sparrow delved deeper into Moseley's pathology. He asked, "Would you consider perpetrating an act of cunnilingus on a dead body rational?" The doctor preferred not to follow him there. Even necrophiliacs were far more common than necrocunnilinguists, but who could say which sort of sexual deviance was more or less rational? Cassino admitted that Moseley's behavior might be bizarre, but insisted that he had followed a step-by-step strategy to achieve his goal. "When the situation brought forth certain unexpected factors, he was able to act upon them with what might be considered good judgment."

"Was it good judgment to go back after persons indicated their presence, and called out after the initial stabbing?"

"I was rather impressed with that," the psychiatrist said. "He waited and looked around. He then saw the coast clear, and went ahead. This represents to me a very considerable capacity to use logic and reason to escape detection for something that he knew, in my opinion, he should not have been doing."

Sparrow pressed on, exploring another topic the prosecution hoped to avoid. Was it rational, he asked, for Moseley to prolong his attack on Kitty after Karl Ross peeked out his doorway and saw him in the act?

Perhaps not, Cassino said. At that moment Ross might have barged out with a gun, or shouted for help, or called the police. But Moseley was carrying out his impulse, finishing what he'd started. According to Dr. Cassino, Moseley had acted rationally in his step-by-step pursuit of his goal, rape and murder. Sparrow shook his head in disbelief. "I have no other questions." At 4:20 p.m. on June 10, the defense rested.

"**W**ith each passing day," Skoller wrote, the crowds in the corridor seemed to grow larger. "The regular court buffs knew summations would take place on June 11th, and that morning the crowd was packed so tightly that it took almost twenty minutes to push through the fifty yards from the elevator to the courtroom door. Reporters were throwing questions without even waiting for answers. 'Do you think the neighbors hurt your case?' 'Will the jury get the case today?' 'Will you push for the death penalty if he is convicted?'" Skoller expected his boss Cacciatore to win the case and persuade the jury to sentence Moseley to death. He wasn't overly worried about the neighbors' apathy, which was more of an issue in the press than in court. He felt as excited as if he were going to a front-row seat at the World Series. "I was told that by the time of the closing arguments, hundreds of spectators spilled outside the courthouse onto Queens Boulevard."

Sparrow spoke first. Relying on M'Naghten, he claimed that Winston Moseley suffered from a defect of reason. "This individual is sick," he said of his client. "I tell you this is a sick, diseased mind, a malfunctioning mind." And what was the mind, Sparrow asked, but a complicated machine? "The most complex machine ever created by God or man, able to create an IBM computer with thousands and thousands of parts, and rockets, spaceships, and this mind is far, far more complex than any of its creations. But what little malfunctioning, what little throwing aside of the gears, makes this mind start going haywire?" According to Sparrow the answers might include a broken home, a lonely childhood, a faithless wife, a bigoted society. The answers might even be unknowable, but the result was a broken machine. The result, he said, pointing to his client, "is this creature who could kill and rape, but who never raises his voice, who never gets excited, who never uses profanity." Sparrow wasn't seeking sympathy for Moseley, he said. He admitted that his client had brutally slain and raped Kitty Genovese, a heinous, hideous act. *But not by choice.* "Cancer is a disease, an illness. So is mental disease. Somewhere down the line the seed was planted in the brain and it grew. He couldn't stop it. He couldn't control it." And if the jurors agreed, they had no choice but to find Winston Moseley not guilty of murder.

In closing, Sparrow urged the jury to strike a blow for human progress. "Insane persons belong in the care of those who are qualified to treat them," he said. "The criminal insane don't belong in jails to rot or in electric chairs to die. We must here today, in this courtroom, strive to attain, through compassionate wisdom, a dignity in our law, and make this a hallmark of our civilization. I ask you, I implore you, when you go into your jury room to deliberate, use such compassionate wisdom. Walk humbly with God, and by compassionate wisdom arrive at that verdict that proves our advances."

Cacciatore took a simpler tack. In the people's summation he said, "A beast roamed the streets of Queens." Looking each juror in the eye he mocked Sparrow's depiction of Moseley as an introvert warped by a troubled youth and revisited Moseley's sex life. "So they do a little variation of the sex act. Cunnilingus," Cacciatore said. "Practice with Pauline a little bit, then it becomes a little better with Betty. This is a *deviation*." He was gathering steam, his voice rising. "They tell you that Moseley is always thinking, always playing with his ants. He played around with an aunt when he was seventeen, and he laid the woman! Oh, excuse me, he had *sexual intercourse*." Finally, lest the jurors forget why they were here, he reminded them of Kitty's ordeal between 3:15 and 4:00 a.m. on the icy morning of March 13, 1964. He wanted them to picture it: How surprised she must have been, locking her car and walking to the corner, to be suddenly attacked from out of nowhere. Stabbed! How brave she was, getting back to her feet after that, with her lung punctured, making her way to a doorway where she could lie down, bleeding, shocked but safe. A place to rest. Until the devil came back to finish what he'd started.

Now, Cacciatore said, the jury had a job to finish. "The people have proven Winston Moseley criminally responsible," he said. "The only verdict justified under the law is: Guilty as charged. Murder in the first degree."

Judge Shapiro gave the jurors their instructions, then sent them out to decide Moseley's fate. Reporters spent the early evening of June 11 trading guesses. How long would the jury take to reach a verdict? Was longer better for Moseley's chances? Had he hurt his defense by seeming so calm on the stand, or helped it by talking about his perverse crimes as if he'd been out running errands? And how about the judge, admitting from the start that he didn't believe in the death penalty? Like any other judge in Queens County, Shapiro had to answer to the voters every election year. Didn't he know that the public wanted Moseley to fry?

After six hours, the jury sent Judge Shapiro a note: *Please give us definition of the various degrees of homicide.*

"That caused a flurry of excitement," one reporter wrote. It suggested that the jurors might have doubts about a first-degree murder verdict. Summoning them back to the courtroom, Shapiro detailed the differences among their four options: first- and second-degree murder, and first- and second-degree manslaughter. Shortly after 10:00 p.m., the jury returned to its deliberations. Several reporters went home.

Ten minutes later, the jurors sent the judge another note: *We have a verdict.*

Again they returned to the jury box. As assistant DA Skoller remembered, "The courtroom grew as quiet as Shea Stadium when the bases are loaded and the ball is sailing toward the plate. The jurors stared straight ahead as they filed into the jury box."

The court clerk addressed them. "Madam and gentlemen of the jury, have you agreed upon a verdict?"

Jury foreman Irving Helfman, a balding accountant, stood up. He said, "We have."

"Defendant rise," Judge Shapiro instructed. "Jurors, look upon the defendant. Defendant, look upon the jurors." Moseley, now wearing black trousers and a white button-down shirt, turned to face Irving Helfman, who said:

"We find the defendant, Winston Moseley, guilty as charged."

15

Consequences

Shapiro's cramped courtroom was jammed on Monday, June 15, for the trial's last stage, the penalty phase, when the jury would decide whether Moseley lived or died. A crowd of at least a thousand overflowed the lobby, the courthouse steps, and the sidewalk, interfering with traffic on Queens Boulevard.

The judge made several key decisions that morning. He allowed the prosecution to call to the stand four women Moseley had molested before he began killing his victims. None had any other connection to the Genovese case. One, Joan Larrinaga, thirty-four, had been surprised in her bedroom by a man with a flashlight. Certain that she was about to be raped, she said, "Please, not in the same room with my baby." Moseley said, "To hell with the damn baby."

Another victim, Atla Morrell, testified that Moseley had held a screwdriver to her throat and forced her to perform oral sex on him despite the difficulty he had maintaining an erection. "He was too small." He managed to rape her, then let her go.

Sidney Sparrow, sitting at the defense table beside his sleepy-eyed client, thought the rape victims' testimony might help his cause. Moseley had spared their lives; maybe the jury would spare his.

Another of Shapiro's rulings took both sides by surprise. "Shapiro didn't permit evidence of mental illness to be introduced in mitigation of a death sentence," Skoller recalled. It was a curious choice. The jury had already heard several psychiatrists testify about Moseley's warped psyche. All Sparrow wanted was to bring a couple of them back for a minute or two in the penalty phase, to reinforce his suggestion that Moseley might be crazy enough to deserve mercy. But Shapiro wouldn't allow it. The jury had decided that the defendant was sane enough to be guilty, he ruled, and that topic was now off-limits.

The defense was out of options. In a last-ditch appeal to the jury Sparrow admitted that he was disgusted by what his client had done to Kitty Genovese on the morning of March 13. Still he saw humanity in Winston Moseley—despite his personal affection for Kitty. "I didn't try this case involving Kitty Genovese objectively, because *I knew Kitty Genovese*," he blurted. "I represented her for years." In fact Sparrow had been Kitty's lawyer in her 1961 trial for booking horse-race bets, a detail he hadn't mentioned in court.

Judge Shapiro, startled, cut him off. "We didn't know about that. That's not in the record," the judge said. Although, of course, it was now—a handful of lines that would become an issue twenty-five years later.

At 11:25 that morning, seven days after the trial began, Shapiro gave the jurors a final instruction. "Your verdict will be one of two:

You can either say the death penalty, or life imprisonment. Your verdict must be unanimous."

Half an hour passed. Then the jurors sent another message to the judge. They were in agreement. They were coming back.

The court clerk addressed jury foreman Helfman at 12:15. "What is your decision?"

Helfman said, "We, the jury, prescribe the death penalty for Winston Moseley."

Reporters ran for the phones in the lobby. "The room erupted in loud spontaneous applause and cheers," the *Daily News* reported in a story headed CROWD APPLAUDS AS QUEENS JURY DOOMS MOSELEY. "Judge Shapiro pounded his gavel to restore order. 'I've never seen anything like this,' said a veteran court officer. Once the clamor settled down and people took their seats again, the judge added his own thoughts. 'I don't believe in capital punishment, but when I see this monster,' he said, 'I wouldn't hesitate to pull the switch myself!'"

Shapiro's declaration triggered a new round of cheering. "Defendant remanded," he said. "The sooner we get him out of Queens County and into the death cell, the better."

No one knew it at the time, but Judge Shapiro probably wasn't telling the whole truth.

Half a century later, Bob Sparrow, the defense attorney's son, still frets about the Moseley trial. "My dad had a tough assignment, trying to save that guy from the electric chair."

While assisting his father on the case, Bob took part in strategy sessions. He says his father knew how difficult it would be to win a not-guilty verdict but was confident about winning the battle of the shrinks. "Our side had two prominent psychiatrists who examined

Moseley and testified that he didn't understand the difference between right and wrong," he says. "Under the M'Naghten rule, that was the whole point of the trial. Then, in rebuttal, the prosecution brings in a psychiatrist, Dr. Cassino, who'd never met the defendant. And this expert witness had the audacity—the balls—to testify in a capital case that Moseley *did* know right from wrong. How? From observing him in court! We gleaned from jurors that they were so turned off by him that they said, 'These shrinks are all worthless,' and threw out the whole panoply of psychiatric testimony."

As for Shapiro's barring the psychiatrists from the penalty phase, Bob Sparrow can only consider it "intriguing." Shapiro, who died in 1985, "was a brilliant jurist—and an avowed opponent of capital punishment. We believed he was intentionally building reversible error into the case. That way, the public would be happy and Moseley could still escape the death penalty. Shapiro could announce, 'I'd pull the switch myself,' a quote that was reported all over the nation and the world, knowing that the reversal would come later, when nobody was looking."

Barry Rhodes agrees with Sparrow. Rhodes, a fast-talking defense lawyer who would represent Moseley on appeal years later, says, "Yeah, I think it was a poison pill, a ruling that Shapiro meant to be reversed. I mean, put yourself in his place. You're a smart, prominent, hard-as-nails judge. The defense claims the killer is off-his-nut crazy, and you rule out psychiatric evidence in the penalty phase? That's cockamamie. A first-year law student would think so. Shapiro was dooming the conviction to reversal." Few judges enjoy being reversed on appeal, but Shapiro was so highly regarded that a reversal "wouldn't hurt him," says Rhodes. "It was the politic thing to do. He had an outraged populace in Queens to deal with. He could say he'd pull the switch himself and get cheers for it, and still get what he wanted in the long run."

Sure enough, the New York Court of Appeals ruled in 1967 that Shapiro should have allowed psychiatric testimony during the penalty phase. Moseley's conviction stood, but the higher court commuted his sentence from death to life in prison. Shapiro's plan—if that was his plan—had worked perfectly, and the reversal made no apparent dent in his reputation. In 1970 Governor Rockefeller promoted Shapiro to the Appellate Division of the New York State Supreme Court.

By then, the events Moseley set in motion in the spring of 1964 had changed dozens of lives. In time they would affect many more.

Betty Moseley wept as armed guards led her husband from Shapiro's courtroom for the last time. So did the killer's mother. Like the celebrating spectators around them, Betty and Fannie believed that Winston Moseley was on his way to a date with Old Sparky. In the weeks that followed, both women visited him on death row. So did Alphonso, who hoped to comfort Winston only to find him as unperturbed as if he had gotten probation.

A month after the trial, Betty accepted a shipment of her husband's clothes: four shirts, the black trousers and jacket he had worn in court, a sweater, a handkerchief, and four pairs of socks. Moseley wrote to her from prison. *I love you. Be a good girl.* The Bankers Trust Company repossessed his white Corvair when his monthly payments lapsed. Betty's visits became less frequent as months became years and she raised their children without him.

Fannie visited her son once a month or more for years. After the appeals court commuted Moseley's sentence and the state transferred him out of Sing Sing, Fannie drove her rattling sedan 350 miles from South Ozone Park to the state prison at Attica.

...

After Kitty's body made the transit from morgue to funeral home to New Canaan's Lakeview Cemetery, her story moved from newspapers and newsweeklies into think pieces, political campaigns, radio and TV programs, and psychological studies. Soon there was a popular book by Abraham Rosenthal, *Thirty-Eight Witnesses: The Kitty Genovese Case*. The only book he ever wrote, the *Times'* editor's impassioned eighty-seven-page account, published less than four months after the crime, promoted his view of her death: Kitty was the girl who died alone while thirty-eight neighbors ignored her. Along with Gansberg's front-page story, *Thirty-Eight Witnesses* depicted Kitty's murder as a symbol of city life at its worst. She became an urban martyr and her neighbors became infamous as monsters of a new type: heartless onlookers who watched a neighbor die because they "didn't want to get involved."

With the 1960s lurching toward race riots, campus protests, crime waves, and still more assassinations—Martin Luther King Jr. in April 1968, Robert Kennedy two months later—Kitty's story fed what Jim Rasenberger of the *Times* called "an anxiety many Americans felt in those strange days as social mores shifted rapidly and New York's murder rate shot off on a three-decade upward trajectory." Her dying had nothing to do with any of that, but in retrospect it seemed to foreshadow the dark days ahead. The *Herald Tribune* launched a "City in Crisis" series in which Jimmy Breslin, thirty-five, and Dick Schaap, thirty, chronicled what a colleague of theirs called "a great city's descent into hell." Breslin and Schaap portrayed a city that was different after Kitty died: "Women carry tear-gas pens in their pocketbooks. Cabdrivers rest iron bars on the front seat next to them. Store owners keep billy clubs next to the cash register. And people enter parks and the subways and side streets of New York, the most important city in the world, only in fear. The fear is justified."

On October 12, 1965, a haggard John Lindsay waved to a crowd of three hundred in Kew Gardens. The patrician congressman from Manhattan's Upper East Side—the representative from the Silk Stocking District, they called him—was running for mayor against Democrat Abe Beame and a Conservative Party upstart, William F. Buckley. Lindsay, a liberal Republican, certainly outwalked his opponents that day. After marching through Little Italy in the annual Columbus Day parade, he spent the afternoon on a walking tour of the Bronx, then slaked his thirst at the Riedy & McShaffrey bar on 165th Street.

"The last time a politician was in here, he didn't buy the house a drink," one barfly said. "Bad luck. He lost." Lindsay laughed and called for a round of shots and beers. "I hope I'm luckier," he said.

It was after dark when Lindsay reached Austin Street in Kew Gardens. The candidate climbed wooden steps to a hastily built platform festooned with red, white, and blue bunting directly over the spot where Moseley attacked Kitty. An aide handed him a microphone. "The tragedy that happened here," Lindsay declared, "demonstrated that indifference to one's neighbors was a conditioned reflex, a disease spread by political machines which thrive on apathy, to perpetuate the myth that the job of governing New York City is hopeless."

The crowd fidgeted. Kitty's neighbors—those who hadn't fled in the neighborhood—had been reading and hearing about what they called the incident or "that night" for a year and a half now. Accustomed to being told they were selfish or worse, they didn't need a limousine liberal from the Upper East Side lecturing them about apathy.

"What the Kitty Genovese story tells us," Lindsay said, "is that something has gone out of the heart and soul of New York. And who's to blame? It's people who say, 'What's the use?' It's people who say, 'Why get involved?'"

A woman in the crowd said, "Not that again. Why's he talking about that?"

Calling for "people-to-people responsibility," Lindsay waved a hand toward the faint streetlamps that stood over the crime scene. "We will *light* this street," he vowed. "Yes, New Yorkers will stand tall and proud again. But only if every citizen is willing to be his brother's keeper. And then the double padlock on the front door will no longer be the symbol of New York City!"

Lindsay went on to win the election, but his luck didn't last. The city's transit workers went on strike on New Year's Day 1966, the new mayor's first day in office, shutting down subway and bus service. Lindsay gamely walked four miles to City Hall from his Upper East Side apartment. "I still think it's a fun city," he said. Ahead lay riots, a debt crisis, "white flight" to the suburbs, and more rounds of labor strife featuring a 1968 sanitation strike that saw the mayor trudging sidewalks piled head-high with steaming, uncollected garbage. Some of the trash caught fire and filled the streets with an unholy odor. As New York's debt, trash, and murder rate mounted, the *Herald Tribune*'s Schaap turned Lindsay's quote into a headline, giving the blighted metropolis a sarcastic new nickname: Fun City.

Mary Ann abandoned her seaside rental in Far Rockaway for an apartment in New Haven, Connecticut, leaving her painting of Kitty behind. Despite her best efforts to keep her year in Kew Gardens in a mental box, news stories and snippets of conversation slipped through her defenses, bringing Kitty to mind. One day she heard Phil Ochs on the radio, singing about a woman attacked by a stranger, a woman "grabbed" and "stabbed" while the neighbors watched from the safety of their apartments.

Ochs, a rabble-rousing folkie who'd played the Interlude Coffee House in their Tudor building between gigs at bigger venues, had been upset by news stories about Kitty's murder. He made '60s-style apathy the subject of his 1967 song "Outside of a Small Circle of Friends." Starting with the woman who was stabbed in plain sight, Ochs moved to other mid-'60s scenes, his insistent voice in counterpoint to the saloon-tune twang of his guitar: selfish Americans ignoring the poor, the oppressed, the overlooked and defenseless.

Mary Ann reached for the radio dial. She liked Ochs but this stung too much. It sent her flashing back to their nights at Folk City and made her think how happy Kitty would have been to have Phil Ochs sing about her for any other reason.

Mary Ann went on to earn a bachelor's degree in psychology at Southern Connecticut State University in New Haven, then completed course work for a master's degree, but she never bothered to pick up her diploma. "After Kitty died I went from thing to thing. It was hard to focus," she says. "I'd lost my faith in people—in everything, really."

The *Times*' Martin Gansberg went on to write about police brutality and an alcohol-free nightclub called Teen Haven, but kept tabs on the Genovese story. A year after Kitty died, Gansberg found Kew Gardens residents still reeling from the clamor his reporting had caused. "The placidity of Kew Gardens was disrupted," he wrote, the passive voice effacing his paper's active role. "Reporters and television cameramen moved in to investigate the question—to find the thirty-eight." A number that conflicted with other reports as well as his story's original headline had now gained the ring of pure truth. Who could doubt the deadly apathy of the thirty-eight? "All the residents deplore the publicity that followed the discovery that none of those who saw the murder in progress called the police," Gansberg wrote in a follow-up article. It was a curious assertion. After all, he hadn't interviewed all the residents of Kew Gardens, some of whom had launched an "anti-apathy campaign" seeking more publicity, not less, as he mentioned elsewhere in the same story. His editor may have had a hand in the line about "all the residents." Rosenthal took a keen interest in stories that touched on the Genovese case.

Knocking on doors near the crime scene in 1965, Gansberg encountered a woman who said, "I don't want to be involved." A college student told him that nothing had changed since the night Kitty died: "We are still apathetic slobs." Gansberg interviewed witness Robert Mozer while he was getting a haircut. Mozer recalled his confusion that night—how he had shouted at Moseley to "leave that girl alone"—but had mistaken murder for the usual late-night ruckus. "I thought they were some kids having fun." Karl Ross had moved to parts unknown, but Gansberg now claimed for the first time that Kitty had spoken to him from the bottom of the stairs: *"Karl, I'm stabbed,' she called up to him. 'Help me.'"*

Andrée Picq, the French stewardess, told Gansberg she had been afraid to go outside at night since the murder. She'd bought a police whistle. Now she opened her window and blew the whistle if she saw anyone skulking around, and hoped she would have time to use it if someone attacked her. She was certain her neighbors wouldn't help. "They wouldn't make a call to the police. They're afraid to help their neighbors and they're afraid of the police." Elaborating on her trial testimony, Picq recalled hearing Kitty's cries and calling the 102nd Precinct. "I tried, I really tried," she said. "But I was gasping for breath and was unable to talk into the telephone." She hung up.

Gansberg also tracked down Sam Koshkin, who had watched the first attack from a sixth-floor window in the West Virginia Apartments. Koshkin had wanted to phone the police. "I didn't let him," his wife told Gansberg. "I told him there must have been thirty calls already." Marjorie Koshkin may have helped seal Kitty's fate. In a line that went unnoticed at the time—"There must have been thirty calls already"—she alluded to a factor that helped explain why no one intervened in time that night in Kew Gardens, a dynamic that would become known as the bystander effect.

After his first-anniversary article appeared in March 1965, Gansberg reported on stories far removed from Rosenthal's beat, but never fully escaped the editor's shadow. It was editor Rosenthal, not Gansberg, who wrote about the case for the Sunday *New York Times Magazine,* brooding over "the disease of apathy." It was almost understandable, he claimed, that "the 38 did not lift the phone while Miss Genovese was being attacked." They were exhibiting a peculiar sort of big-city apathy that was "almost a matter of psychological survival, if one is surrounded and pressed by millions of people, to prevent them from constantly impinging on you, and the only way to do this is to ignore them." He had witnessed such apathy in Calcutta and felt it casting its shadow over New York, until "Kitty returned in death to cry the city awake." It was Rosenthal, not Gansberg, who published his influential book, *Thirty-Eight Witnesses,* a mere month after Moseley was convicted. "There are, it seems to me, only two logical ways to look at the story of the murder of Catherine Genovese," he wrote on the book's final page. "One is the way of the neighbor on Austin Street—'Let's forget the whole thing.' The other is to recognize that the bell tolls even on each man's individual island, to recognize that every man must fear the witness in himself who whispers to close the window."

Rosenthal was a complex character. "When he was happy, it glowed through every particle of his face," Gay Talese wrote. "When he was miserable, his face floundered with despair or erupted with emotion." A true believer in the American dream that he believed he was living, Rosenthal was a Cold War hawk. He could be a bully, and *Times* writers considered him a homophobe. Upon returning from overseas in 1963 he had noticed a growing number of "obvious homosexuals" in New York. He assigned what Charles Kaiser, author of *The Gay Metropolis*, called "the kind of story he would become famous for: a huge, attention-getting account that purported to tell the reader everything he needed to know about a particular subject." The story appeared on the front page three months before Kitty was killed. Headed GROWTH OF HOMOSEXUALITY IN CITY PROVOKES WIDE CONCERN, it told of "homosexual haunts" in Greenwich Village and elsewhere in a city with "what is probably the greatest homosexual population in the world . . . the subject of growing concern of psychiatrists, religious leaders, and the police." Noting the "tendency of homosexuals to be promiscuous and seek pick-ups," the five-thousand-word article (Talese deemed it "superb") cited "many experts" who affirmed that the scourge of sexual inversion "can be both prevented and cured." One can only wonder whether Rosenthal would have felt differently about Kitty if he had known that she was one of the Village's sexual inverts.

Protected by the clout of the world's premier newspaper, the Pulitzer Prize–winning editor, who became assistant managing editor in 1967, downplayed coverage that questioned U.S. policy in Vietnam. Later he blocked stories on the city's AIDS crisis. But Rosenthal could also be something close to heroic. Fifteen years after the Genovese case, when the *Times* had to decide whether to publish the Pentagon Papers—leaked documents disproving the United States' official version of the Vietnam War—it was flag-waver Rosenthal who made the call to publish. ("This stuff is really going to help people that I don't agree with," he said, "but that's that. You can't worry about it.") Yet he didn't hesitate to bigfoot Martin Gansberg on the Genovese story. He considered himself the real authority on Kitty Genovese. According to one insider, "Abe Rosenthal actually put his own name on the Pulitzer Prize application" for Gansberg's article. "The Pulitzer committee didn't know what to make of that." The Pulitzer Prize Office at Columbia University confirms that the *Times* nominated both Gansberg and Rosenthal for the prize in Local Investigative Specialized Reporting that year, for the front-page story that ran under Gansberg's byline. Though it wasn't announced at the time, the story was not among the three finalists for the award.

"My father wasn't a prideful man," says Alan Gansberg, the reporter's son. "He never patted himself on the back, but he was proud of his work on the Kitty Genovese story. He thought it was wrong that A. M. Rosenthal wrote a book on the case that barely mentioned him." Anthologies featuring Gansberg's 1964 front-page story filled a bookshelf in the reporter's home. A plaque on the wall commemorated his 1964 award from the Newspaper Reporters' Association of New York. He kept a cardboard box full of prizes and citations including several "Best News Article of the Year" awards.

Many award-winning reporters get promoted. Gansberg, who worked for the *Times* until 1985, was relegated to working on special sections—travel guides, recipes, and the like. His last position was assistant regional editor in New Jersey. He died in 1995. "He wasn't the type to brood," his son says. Still, Martin Gansberg never forgave Rosenthal for stealing the story that would outlive them both.

16

Calling for Help

The first telephone call was a call for help. Alexander Graham Bell had spent months trying to decide how a telephone call should begin. He knew that callers shouldn't just start talking without knowing if they were being heard. But what word or words would signal that a call was under way? Bell chose *Ahoy*, and that's how telephone calls began in the year after his invention—until Thomas Edison suggested *Hello*. But on the very first phone call, on March 10, 1876, eighty-seven years before Kitty called Mary Ann on the pay phone behind the Ansonia Hotel, Bell forgot all about *Ahoy*. After spilling battery acid on his lap he leaned toward his experimental apparatus and called to his assistant, *Mr. Watson, come here—I want to see you!*

In 1956 the National Association of Fire Chiefs recommended that cities employ a single number for people to call when disaster struck. Police departments in Canada used 999, which was easy to remember but took forever to dial on a rotary phone. Chicagoans could call PO5-1313, the *PO* for "Police." Other American cities used other numbers. In 1964, as Martin Gansberg reported in the *Times*, the Kitty Genovese case spurred New York police and politicians to join the push for a single emergency number to replace the borough and precinct numbers then on the books. Three years later the Federal Communications Commission and the Bell System announced that they would team up to select a number all Americans could remember and dial in a hurry.

The result came in January 1968. Bell announced that the national emergency number would be 911. It was easy to remember and simple to dial, with an initial 9 that suited the quirks of Bell's switching systems. Phone company officials looked forward to a ballyhooed rollout of their innovation later that year—until three men in Alabama beat them to the punch.

B. W. Gallagher, president of the Alabama Telephone Company and a competitive son of a gun, read about the Bell System's plan in the *Wall Street Journal*. Gallagher thought, *Why wait?* He enlisted an employee, technical whiz Robert Fitzgerald, to engineer a 911 call in Haleyville, population 4,500. After a month of preparations featuring plenty of sparks, crossed wires, late nights, and elbow grease, state and local leaders gathered at Haleyville's red-brick City Hall. Rankin Fite, Speaker of the Alabama House of Representatives, dialed the three digits from a telephone on the mayor's desk. Engineer Fitzgerald, standing by in a switching station between City Hall and the town's jail, watched mechanical switches fall into place. A nine, a one, a one. An instant later the telephone in the Haleyville police chief's office, a cherry-red rotary phone, rang. U.S. Representative Tom Bevill was waiting. Beside Bevill sat Theophilus Eugene "Bull" Connor, the Birmingham police chief who had turned attack dogs and fire hoses on civil-rights marchers four years before and still joked about it. ("My dogs wouldn't bite the niggers till I gave 'em a bath," he said.) Now wheelchair-bound after a stroke, Connor smiled as Congressman Bevill picked up the red receiver and said, "Hello."

That was the beginning and the end of America's first 911 call. Bevill hung up, and then the politicians went out for coffee and doughnuts.

The transformative year 1968 also saw the publication of a landmark report by sociologists Bibb Latané of Ohio State University and John Darley of Princeton. Drawn to their topic of Kitty's murder, Latané and Darley began their monograph, *The Unresponsive Bystander*, by citing a tenet of social interaction known as the Threefold Cord, which traditionally bound each member of society to his or her neighbors, providing "succor, warmth and mutual defense." Echoing many reports on the murder, they noted a growing feeling in the turbulent '60s that "present-day society is fragmented, that compassion is disappearing, old moralities crumbling." The Threefold Cord was stretched to the snapping point. With a nod toward Rosenthal's *Thirty-Eight Witnesses* they asked whether modern life had brought forth a new species of detached, hard-hearted human: *Homo urbanis*.

Latané and Darley wondered what, if anything, could spur urban Americans to get involved in their neighbors' lives. They began with low-risk social science experiments in which college students asked random New Yorkers for directions, or offered them candy, or courted trouble by tossing Frisbees around Grand Central Station. Most bystanders reacted with suspicion or pretended not to notice.

Latané and Darley pushed further by staging scenarios that seemed to pose physical risk to those who intervened, even life-and-death risk. In almost every case they found an unexpected common thread: "A very important factor in the amount of responsibility felt by any one bystander," they wrote, "is the number of other people he thinks are present and available to help."

Or as Marjorie Koshkin put it when her husband reached for the phone, "There must have been thirty calls already."

According to *The Unresponsive Bystander*, "The number of people who stand and watch is what shocks us; it also may be the key to their behavior." While the number of witnesses "determines to a very important degree what they will do, it does so in a way opposite to what is usually assumed. The presence of others serves to inhibit the impulse to help." Rather than strength in numbers, weakness.

In one experiment a young woman brought test subjects into a classroom to take a questionnaire, then retreated behind a curtain. The subjects heard a crash, followed by her cries of "Oh my God, my foot. My ankle! I can't get . . . this thing . . . off me." If a subject was alone in the room, the researchers found, he or she went to help the woman 70 percent of the time. But when subjects were among others—actors who feigned disinterest—they took action only 7 percent of the time.

Adding a villain raised the stakes. Experimenters sent a "thief" to steal an envelope full of money off a classroom desk. Many witnesses fidgeted, but most pretended that nothing had happened. Subjects who had clearly watched the theft claimed later that they had seen nothing. Latané and Darley reasoned that people under stress make subconscious calculations. If a bystander can see no evil or hear no evil, like the questionnaire-takers who heard a crash behind a curtain, "he need not worry about feeling guilty for sitting still, or making a fool of himself for jumping up. He can relax."

Their work suggested a social dynamic that may have worked against Kitty on her final night. Diffusion of responsibility, they called it—a phenomenon that distributed guilt like a firing squad in reverse. If one person sees trouble, "he will feel all the guilt for not acting. If others are present, responsibility is diffused, and the finger of blame points less directly at any one person."

To test their theory, Latané and Darley designed an emergency "to resemble Kitty Genovese's murder." Experimental subjects were asked to wait for instructions relayed by loudspeaker from the next room. After a few moments a voice over the speaker (provided by one of many underemployed actors the researchers found in New York) seemed to go off script. "Oh. Uh, uh," the "instructor" said, pretending to suffer a seizure. "I could really use some help. If somebody would . . . uh, I'm gonna die. Help." There were choking sounds, then silence.

The social scientists had conspicuously posted an assistant in the hallway. To help the dying instructor, subjects needed only to inform the assistant. How many did? The answer depends on how much company they thought they had. Some had been told there were four other subjects awaiting instructions in other rooms. Some had been told there was one other subject. Some had been told they were the only one. And that made all the difference: Eighty-five percent of those who believed they were the sole listener told the assistant that something was wrong—the "instructor" needed help. Sixty-two percent of those who thought there was one other listener did the same. But the percentage plummeted for those who thought they were part of a group: of those who believed they were among five subjects, only 31 percent took action. Despite hearing gasps and explicit pleas for help, more than two out of three sat still, pretending not to hear what they heard.

The Unresponsive Bystander suggested that the tragedy of the Genovese case wasn't that dozens of people witnessed Moseley's attack on

Kitty, but that more than one or two did. If the psychologists were right, most of us can summon the courage to act if there is no one else who could do so, but not when there are others who might take action. If somebody else is in a position to help—someone who might be stronger, braver, or more level-headed—we want him or her to go first. Even if we only think or hope others might help, we expect them to go first.

Not that we plan or even *decide* to sit still when someone needs help. When the experimenters asked subjects why they ignored a seizure victim's distress, they said they "didn't know what to do" or "didn't know what was happening." None reported feeling a lessened sense of responsibility. Asked whether knowing there were other "witnesses" had affected them, they all said no. Latané and Darley concluded that the bystander effect works subconsciously. They closed their report by calling for a more nuanced look at so-called urban apathy. "Glib phrases may contain some truth, since startling cases such as the Genovese murder often occur in our large cities," they wrote. "But our studies suggest a different conclusion. They suggest that situational factors may be of greater importance. The failure to intervene may be better understood by knowing the relationship among bystanders than that between a bystander and the victim."

Experiments like theirs couldn't happen today. Universities and other research institutions, hamstrung by fears of legal liability, don't dare expose subjects to challenges like hearing a seizure victim plead for help. What if a test subject had a stress-related panic attack? Or heart attack? Or felt so ashamed of ignoring the victim's pleas that he sued for mental cruelty or loss of self-esteem? But in the years following Latané and Darley's path-breaking work, a Fordham study showed that hundreds of New York City pedestrians would ignore a man breaking into a parked car. A Penn State researcher who restaged Kitty's plight in multiple variations found that when the young woman said, "Get away! I don't know you," bystanders helped her 65 percent of the time. When she said, "Get away! I don't know why I ever married you," they helped her 19 percent of the time.

The bystander effect, also known as Genovese syndrome, led City University of New York professor Herbert Kaufman to pioneer a field he dubbed "prosocial behavior." Kaufman sought ways to turn bad Samaritans into good neighbors. Another researcher, Stanley Milgram—a Harvard and CUNY professor famed for the "Peer Shock" experiment in which Milgram's subjects delivered (fake) electric shocks to strangers—made the Genovese case a touchstone for the field he called urban psychology. According to Fordham professor Harold Takooshian, a protégé of Milgram's, Kitty's murder became the wellspring for "three fields that barely existed before the Genovese case," urban psychology, social psychology, and the study of prosocial behavior.

Takooshian calls Kitty's murder "the most-cited incident in social psychology literature until the September 11 attacks of 2001." Another social psychologist, Penn State's R. Lance Shotland, told the *Times* that between 1964 and 1984 "more than a thousand articles and books attempted to explain the behavior of bystanders in crises." That was more than the number devoted to the Holocaust over the same twenty years.

Understanding why bystanders hesitate to act hasn't helped victims who came after Kitty: Cheryl Araujo, gang-raped in a bar in a 1984 case retold in the Jodie Foster film *The Accused*; Angel Arce, run over by a car in Hartford, Connecticut, and ignored by scores of drivers and bystanders, some of whom told police that they "didn't want to get involved"; two-year-old Axel Casian, stomped to death by his father while a Turlock, California, crowd looked on; Esmin Green, who collapsed at Kings County Hospital in Brooklyn in 2008 and died after lying on the waiting-room floor for more than an hour; a fifteen-year-old California schoolgirl gang-raped during homecoming while other students watched; Hugo Tale-Yax of Queens, stabbed in the chest while saving a woman from a knife-wielding thug in 2010, bleeding to death while pedestrians walked by, one pausing to snap a cell phone photo; and many others whose misfortunes never made news. Each year new victims fall afoul of what criminologists have called an open secret of city life: the fact that criminals often commit crimes in public because they know witnesses won't challenge them. Still Takooshian sees signs of progress. Every crime that reminds people of the Genovese case, whether it occurs in a Connecticut tavern, on a Chinese street, or a London sidewalk, renews discussion of her case, her name, and the fraught dynamic of victim and witness. Kitty's suffering led to "national soul-searching and more," says Takooshian.

The 911 emergency phone system may be the most familiar reform, but there are others that go well beyond the sodium-arc streetlamps the Lindsay administration planted on New York's sidewalks after Lindsay promised to "light this street." In the years after the Genovese case, many states enacted "Good Samaritan" laws encouraging witnesses to stop crime or at least report it. California, Florida, Massachusetts, and seven other states passed duty-to-aid laws obliging citizens to help others in need if they could do it without putting themselves in danger. Kitty's name has been linked to these and other reforms including victim- and witness-assistance programs, laws allowing victims to speak in felony trials' penalty phases, crime-victim compensation, sex-offender registries, neighborhood watch groups, and grassroots efforts to fight crime all over the United States. The soul-searching prompted by her murder led countless Americans to consider their duty to others. In the late '60s future Supreme Court justice Sonia Sotomayor, then a debater at Cardinal Spellman High School in the Bronx, entered a contest with a speech on the Genovese case. "We must not forget that we are a community," young Sotomayor argued. She won the contest.

Due to its prominence in social-psychology studies, the Genovese case may have played at least an indirect role in the events of September 11, 2001. On that Tuesday morning, four al-Qaeda terrorists hijacked United Airlines Flight 93 over Ohio. They killed the pilot and slit a flight attendant's throat. The hijackers turned the plane east, planning to crash into the White House or the U.S. Capitol. They expected the passengers to stay in their seats and follow instructions. Instead, some passengers refused to be bystanders. By then millions of Americans had encountered the Genovese case in psychology textbooks. Todd Beamer, Mark Bingham, Tom Burnett, and Jeremy Glick may or may not have been among them; in any case their action embodied the prosocial behavior that academics used the case to promote—the opposite of "I don't want to get involved." (Beamer was heard on an open phone line, saying, "Are you guys ready? Okay, let's roll.") Together, the four men charged the terrorists. The heroes of Flight 93 died along with the hijackers when the plane crashed in an empty field near Shanksville, Pennsylvania, but by fighting back they saved the lives of dozens if not hundreds of strangers on the ground.

In 2009, US Airways pilot Chesley "Sully" Sullenberger saved 155 passengers and crew by guiding his disabled 400-ton Airbus to a miracle landing in the Hudson River. Sullenberger had been a middle-school student in Denison, Texas, in 1964, when he first heard about Kitty's death. He asked himself how New Yorkers could be so cold. "I made a pledge to myself right then and there, at age thirteen, that if I was ever in a situation where someone such as Kitty Genovese needed my help, I would choose to act. No one in danger would be abandoned," he recalled. In the hour after his "Miracle on the Hudson," as Sullenberger and his passengers stood shivering on the plane's wing while boaters rushed to help, he felt as if New York was "reaching out to warm us."

17

Jailbreak

J udge Irwin Shapiro's "poison pill" saved Winston Moseley's life. The judge's decision to bar psychiatric testimony in the penalty phase of his trial, a decision that was promptly overturned on appeal, led Moseley to a bunk at the super-maximum-security Attica State Prison instead of the Rosenbergs' seat on Old Sparky at Sing Sing.

Rather than electrocute the prisoner, the State of New York put him through a battery of tests. Electroencephalogram: normal. IQ test: 112 with a verbal score of 118, not as high as his pretrial performance but still in the "bright intellectual" range. An examiner described Moseley as "polite, cautious, cooperative." A confidential psychiatric report categorized him as an introvert and a "compulsive personality—meticulous, careful, exacting in many details of his everyday life. Possibly incipient schizophrenic." Apparently adept at walling off or shutting off his emotions, he was "psychologically very well defended."

A model prisoner, the quiet lifer spent his days playing ping-pong with other inmates or reading in the prison library. Sometimes, brooding over his life sentence, he retreated to his cell and slept for long stretches. One state-appointed psychiatrist who interviewed him, Dr. Jess Charles, reported feeling a chill when he sat down with Moseley. "He is a small, effeminate-appearing male. His facial expression is flattened, inappropriate at times," Charles noted in a confidential memo. "He appears to be a 'cold fish.' Presumably this borderline schizophrenic has been so exquisitely sensitive that in order to survive he has repressed the emotional aspect of his life to such an extent that he can't 'feel.' He is cut off from the thing that makes him human. In my opinion it is beside the point whether he is severely schizoid, borderline schizophrenic, or just plain schizophrenic. The point is, I believe society needs continuing protection from this man."

Moseley wrote hundreds of letters from prison, all in a precise, flowing script with each line and margin on the unlined paper carefully spaced, each word carefully drawn. He wrote to Betty, Fannie, Alphonso, lawyers, wardens and other corrections officials, complaining about boredom and racism in prison, asking for visits, magazines, a radio. He closed his letters with a flowery signature in which the *M* of his surname trailed into a curlicue and the final *y* spun into a showy double whirl. It was the penmanship of a performer.

In one letter Moseley described himself as "a respected and trusted prisoner" forced to endure Attica's "rigorous discipline, continuous brutality, virulent racism, and homosexuality." He wanted out. Soon after arriving at Attica in 1967, he admitted later, he began considering what he called "a desperate expedient." Escape.

After breakfast on March 12, 1968, four years to the day after he went hunting for a white girl to kill, he told a guard that he was experiencing some discomfort. It was discomfort of a private sort, he said, indicating the seat of his pants. Later that morning Dr. Selden Williams, senior physician at Attica, examined inmate Moseley and found that he had an object lodged in his rectum. The object was a meat tin of the sort that held Spam—he had bought it in the prison commissary. Three inches wide, about an inch and a half high, it was lodged "one to two inches down inside the rectum," slick with blood, feces, and bits of a plastic bag. Williams couldn't imagine how he had plunged such an object so far into his anus. "I can't really understand how the heck he ever inserted it," the doctor recalled. The pain had to be excruciating, but other than a few slight winces as Williams examined him, Moseley seemed as calm as ever.

After putting him under a general anesthetic, Williams and his medical team tried to extract the can. They used clamps, tweezers, and fingers on the unconscious patient. "I was able to get my hand behind the can and wiggle it around, but couldn't remove it," the doctor reported. "After three-quarters of an hour we had quite a bit of bleeding. I felt he belonged in a general hospital, so I terminated my efforts and called Meyer Memorial" in Buffalo. Just as Moseley had hoped.

Surgeons at E. J. Meyer Memorial Hospital removed the tin can, and the patient recovered quickly. Six days later, on March 18, he was ready for the thirty-five-mile ride back to Attica. Two prison guards were dispatched to pick him up in a state-owned Ford station wagon. Only one of them was armed. Herman "Hy" Spencer, fifty-six, a chubby corrections-department veteran with a snub-nosed .32 pistol on his hip, signed in at the hospital, taking legal possession of the pajama-clad prisoner, who sat in a wheelchair. Moseley must have been sore so soon after rectal surgery. Corrections officer Spencer wheeled him to a dressing room, where the inmate laboriously removed his pajamas and put on his gray prison uniform. He bent over to tie his shoes, then lunged for the door.

"He bolted up, knocked me off-balance," Spencer recalled. After that, "everything happened so fast." Moseley knocked the guard off his feet and fled into the hallway, where he ran to the nearest exit.

In Spencer's account, "I immediately regained my composure and went outside" in time to see Moseley sprinting toward a stand of pine trees. "I called his name, told him to halt, and fired one warning shot." Moseley kept running.

Puffing through the parking lot, Spencer passed a pedestrian. "Are you looking for a Negro, running?" the man asked.

"Yes!"

"He just went over the fence."

M oseley slipped through traffic on Buffalo's Kensington Expressway, climbed another fence, and hurried west on Dewey Avenue. There was a little house in the middle of the block with no car in the driveway or the garage. He broke a cellar window and crawled inside. By then corrections officer Spencer had given up the chase. Returning to the station wagon, he radioed news of the escape to his superiors at Attica as well as the state police, Buffalo police, and Erie County Sheriff's Department. In minutes the manhunt was on, a search that would set police officers in sixteen states on the trail of a fugitive Erie County's district attorney described as "a vicious animal."

Moseley settled into his hideout nine hundred yards from the hospital. The house was stuffy and dusty, unoccupied for three years, but it must have felt roomy to a man who had spent four years in prison cells. Ransacking closets, drawers, and cabinets, he found little canned food, a pocket knife, and, to his delight, a loaded .45 caliber revolver. He holed up in his safe house while the city buzzed with false sightings of the escaped convict news reports described as "fugitive killer" and "Genovese slayer" Winston Moseley. Buffalo cops and state troopers followed up dozens of tips that led nowhere.

After three days of lying low, Moseley tried the phone. He was surprised to get a dial tone. He called the New York State Employment Service and said, "Please send a maid." He'd be happy to pay, he said. "Send her right away." The service dispatched a young black woman, Zella Moore, who drove the mile from her green-shingled Buffalo home to the quiet house on Dewey Avenue, across the expressway from the hospital. She rang the bell. A thin, soft-spoken man invited her in. The man waited while she cleaned the house, then threatened her with the gun he'd found. "Do what I say or I'll shoot you." Over the next five hours, while Zella Moore pleaded for her life, saying she had children waiting at home, Moseley raped her. Finally, warning her not to tell anyone where to find him, he let her go.

The anguished cleaning woman wasn't about to call the police. She didn't trust them. She was afraid Moseley might get away again and track her down. At the same time she didn't want somebody else walking into that house. The employment service gave her a phone number for the homeowner, Janet Kulaga, a medical technician at Buffalo General Hospital whose parents had lived in the Dewey Avenue house until her father died. Moore called Kulaga. "There's something funny going on in that house," she said.

Kulaga didn't think it sounded funny. Her mother had left some of her possessions in the house—including a handgun—and now the cleaning lady was panicked, talking about "apples and orange peels on the floor, and one of the beds looked like it was slept in," but refusing to say much more except "I'm not going back. Don't let your mother go in there."

Police logs at Buffalo's 16th Precinct show that an officer took Janet Kulaga's call shortly after 7:00 a.m. on March 21. (The city was switching to a 911 system, but the transition wouldn't be complete until 1988.) Kulaga said she was worried about "something funny" at her parents' empty house. Somebody seemed to be living there. Could a police officer meet her at 278 Dewey?

"Sorry," said the duty officer. There was a shift change coming up. "The next shift comes on at eight-thirty. If you call back, somebody could meet you then."

Kulaga didn't want to wait. She and her husband, Mathew, drove to the house on Dewey Avenue. They had heard radio reports of a killer on the loose but paid little attention. But when they saw the shattered cellar window, Mathew took a crowbar from his car to use as a weapon, just in case. Matt Kulaga was a forty-year-old research chemist; he didn't think of himself as a tough guy, but this house belonged to him and his wife. Police or no police, they weren't going to let a squatter or a bunch of partying teenagers treat the place like a motel.

Janet Kulaga used her mother's keys to open the side door. The Kulagas' eyes were still adjusting to the half light inside when they came face-to-face with Winston Moseley. He stood in the shadows at the top of a short flight of stairs, aiming the family .45 at them. Matt Kulaga dropped the crowbar.

Moseley's voice was soft. Reasonable. "Come on in. I won't hurt you." He led them to the living room, where the three of them sat on the couch while Moseley went through Janet's purse and Matt's wallet. He pocketed thirty-one dollars. "Now let's go upstairs." He followed them, gun in hand.

When they reached a bedroom, he ordered Matt to strip. Once Matt was down to his underwear, Moseley turned to Janet. "Tie him up," he said. He had a tangle of clothesline stashed nearby. After cutting several lengths with the pocketknife he had found, he tossed them to her, but Janet wasn't up to the task. Her hands shook. So their captor expertly bound and gagged her husband—wrists tied behind his back, ankles bound, a wad of wet cotton in Matt's mouth, a strip of towel tied over his mouth and knotted behind the back of his head. These were not skills that Moseley had possessed as a Remington Rand operator. Four years in prison had educated him.

Janet stood beside the bed, still fully dressed. Moseley gagged her. He tied her hands, leaving her ankles free so that she could walk to the next bedroom. Around this time he mentioned that he was "Moseley, the escaped killer."

Matt lay facedown and hogtied on his mother-in-law's bed, listening. He heard nothing. After five to ten minutes, his captor returned and pulled down the shades. What had Moseley done to Janet? Raped her? Killed her? Matt heard clothes rustling. He heard the clink of a belt buckle, his own belt buckle. There was enough light to see Moseley dressing in Matt's pants, sport coat, shirt, and tie. When he finished knotting the tie, he could have passed for a schoolteacher. Or a chemist.

"How far is it to New York City?"

He loosened the gag enough for Matt to mumble, "About four hundred miles." Matt was too afraid to ask about his wife.

Then Moseley was gone. A minute later, Matt heard his car start outside. The car was a 1962 Mercury Comet, white, the size and color of the Corvair the killer had left behind in South Ozone Park. Moseley backed down the driveway to Dewey Avenue and headed for the New York State Thruway.

The house was quiet. Matt struggled with his bonds. It took several minutes to work his hands free. He untied his feet and stumbled to the next room, where his wife lay spread-eagled on the bed.

Moseley had lashed Janet's ankles to opposite bedposts. Just as he had done with Kitty, he'd sliced open her bra with his knife. He had sucked her nipples and proceeded to rape her, but couldn't keep his erection. The attack was over sooner than the attacker wanted it to be. Janet was telling her husband all this while Matt untied her. She said Moseley had stood up after raping her, had covered her breasts with her blouse, and offered to help her put her slacks back on. Still gagged, she shook her head no. Moseley reached for her hand. He took a diamond engagement ring and a white-gold wedding band off Janet's fingers. Then he reached toward her again. "Before he left the bedroom," she said, "he patted me on the head and told me he hoped I'd never have another experience like this."

For the second time that day, the Kulagas phoned the police. This time the duty officer sent a car. Detectives Mickey Chernetsky and Joe Schwartz interviewed the haggard Kulagas, showing them mug shots of Moseley and other men. Both detectives had been part of the three-day multistate manhunt for Moseley. Chernetsky knew the Kitty Genovese case from a psychology class he had taken at Buffalo State College, and like many who read about Kitty he wished he could have been in Kew Gardens to help her. His heart leaped when the Kulagas pointed at Moseley's photo and said, "That's him!"

Moseley was weaving through traffic on the thruway. Suddenly free, armed, and dangerous, zipping along in the Kulagas' Comet with open road ahead, he took a wrong turn and wound up on Grand Island, a flat, teardrop-shaped island ten minutes south of Niagara Falls. At that point, rather than continue to Ontario or circle back toward New York, he pulled over outside the garden apartment of Mary Kay Patmos, who was alone with her five-month-old daughter.

Moseley forced his way in. Minutes later a visitor arrived: Gladys Costanzo, who worked with Patmos at a local church nursery. Moseley yanked her inside. Now he had three hostages.

"They'll miss us at church," Costanzo told him. "They'll start calling and looking for us."

Moseley waved the .45. "If I let you go and you tell anyone, I'll kill your friend and her baby."

Costanzo promised not to tell.

Moseley knew the police would be looking for the white Comet. "Bring me a car," he told her. With a last vow to kill Patmos and the baby if Costanzo double-crossed him, he let her go.

She drove to the church and phoned her husband, who phoned the FBI. Within two hours, scores of federal, state, and local lawmen were taking positions outside the Patmos apartment, keeping their heads down to stay out of sight. State troopers sealed off the two bridges that connected Grand Island to the rest of the world.

Neil Welch, the special agent in charge of the FBI office in Buffalo, commanded the police and federal agents on the scene. Welch, forty-two, a bulldog-faced G-man in a Popeye Doyle fedora, later earned the nickname Jaws for the way he snapped at slow-thinking underlings. After spending much of the '60s in the South ("We tried to keep the Ku Klux Klan in line"), he was seen as a potential successor to J. Edgar Hoover as the bureau's director. When someone asked about Welch's hobbies, he said, "What are hobbies?"

With Welch running the show, the crowd of armed law officers surrounding the apartment grew to more than two hundred. They watched Gladys Costanzo return, as she had promised Moseley. Costanzo parked, placed a set of keys on the car's roof, and walked away. All Moseley had to do was come out and drive into the sunset. But he didn't take the bait. Sensing a trap, he stayed inside, peeking out the window at an empty street.

He was right—the keys were fake.

Long minutes passed as nobody moved. Then Welch decided that there had already been enough screwing around. He phoned the Patmos apartment. Moseley picked up.

"You're surrounded," Welch said. "Come out."

Instead, Kitty's killer hung up. He looked out the front window and saw Welch on the sidewalk beside a state police captain, Erie County's sheriff, and the city's chief of detectives. Moseley raised one finger. *Only one of you.* Then he pointed at Welch.

He let Special Agent Welch through the front door. Welch entered alone, the door slapping shut behind him. Moseley, meticulous as ever, locked the door and fastened the chain lock before leading Welch inside.

The two men sat in a dark living room. Moseley seemed to prefer dim light. Welch was wearing a new pair of prescription glasses that day, his first bifocals, and he kept trying to find a clear image of Moseley above or below the horizontal line in his lenses. He urged Moseley to give up—"There's no way out of this"—while Kitty's killer used one hand to sip from a bottle of Coca-Cola. With his other hand he trained the Kulagas' .45 on the spot between Welch's lenses. He said he would never surrender. He'd die first. Welch kept him talking while Mary Patmos crept to a rear window in another room, handed her toddler to the police outside, then climbed out herself.

Now Moseley and Welch were alone. Both were armed, though Welch had his service revolver hidden in the pocket of his overcoat. "There I was with this psychopath son of a bitch pointing a gun at my head," he recalled later, "while I kept my hand on the gun in my pocket."

They talked for almost an hour. Moseley did most of the talking, recalling his travels, most of them involuntary, from Harlem to Michigan, Detroit, Pittsburgh, South Ozone Park, Sing Sing, and finally Attica, where men were treated like animals. Welch told him what would happen when he surrendered, making it sound inevitable: Nobody would hurt him. Welch would drive him to the station himself with no muss, no bruises. After a while Moseley mentioned the TV show *The F.B.I.*, starring Efrem Zimbalist Jr. as a no-nonsense agent who reminded him of Welch. Who reminded him of the FBI agent the young Winston Moseley dreamed of being. Now he watched the show at Attica, where other inmates rooted for the bad guys. "I like that show," he said.

The phone rang. Somehow neither man's trigger finger twitched. Welch answered and found himself talking to a TV reporter asking for an update: Did he think the hostage crisis would be over in time for the evening news?

Welch *almost* thought that was funny. He told Moseley, "The television guys are out there. So why don't you cut the crap?"

After a long breath, Moseley set the .45 on the table between them.

They left together. Welch led his smirking prisoner through the front door, past a phalanx of cops, news photographers, and TV crews to a waiting car. G-man Welch got most of the attention, but he made a point of sharing the spotlight with two Buffalo cops. Moseley's right wrist was handcuffed to Detective Schwartz. His left wrist was cuffed to Detective Chernetsky, the one who had studied the Kitty Genovese case.

A reporter asked Welch how he managed to keep his cool in a showdown with a killer like Moseley. "How do you talk to a guy like that?"

Welch said, "Very carefully."

18

Memory and Myth

Moseley's escape led the New York State Commission of Correction and the warden at Attica to reform the way they moved convicts from place to place. From then on, teams of armed guards transported inmates to and from hospitals, and the inmates were handcuffed.

An Erie County grand jury reprimanded the Buffalo Police Department for failing to respond to Janet Kulaga's first call. The grand jury also scolded poor Zella Moore for keeping Moseley's hideout a secret, declaring, "We recommend that all private citizens recognize their moral, if not legal, responsibility to advise law enforcement of the whereabouts of wanted criminals and of criminal activity." Janet and Matt Kulaga sued the state for $1.25 million, charging that the correction department shouldn't have let Moseley escape. They lost when a Court of Claims judge agreed that the state had been negligent but ruled that it wasn't liable for damages, due to contributory negligence on the Kulagas' part. "They were not innocent bystanders," the judge wrote. After being warned of "something funny going on," hearing radio reports of a killer on the loose, and seeing signs of a break-in, they "assumed the risks and contributed to the events they complain of" by entering the house where the killer was hiding.

Moseley settled back into prison life at Attica. He lobbied for personal attention, peppering the warden's office with letters penned in his filigreed hand. One typical letter complained about the handling of his mail. The prisoner insisted that he had sent his mother money that never reached her, and said that magazines he ordered— *Ebony, Jet, Hustler*—never made it to his cell. His tone was deferential. "I have never had anything against this place personally, and though I may not agree with the idea of jail in principle, I'm far from what might be called a troublemaker," he claimed in a letter to the warden less than a year after his escape and recapture. "I will not participate in anything that does not serve an instructive purpose."

In 1971 came the notorious riot that saw inmates seize control of the prison. Governor Rockefeller sent state police to quell the uprising at Attica. Twenty-nine prisoners died along with ten of their hostages. "A trial of fire and death," Moseley wrote of the riot. "I vowed then and there that I was going to make amends for my past wrongdoing." Full of hope for his future, he applied for a furlough in 1975. He was naive; furlough was a pipedream for such a notorious killer. Undeterred, he began a long campaign to prove that he would deserve parole when he became eligible in 1984. The soft-spoken murderer excelled in typing classes. He served as vice president and then president of Attica's inmate liaison committee, conducting meetings with prison officials. He took correspondence courses from Niagara University, got straight As, and in 1977 earned a bachelor's degree in sociology, becoming the first convicted murderer in state history to earn a college degree from his cell. Later that year the *Times* published an editorial by Moseley on its op-ed page. Under the headline *I'M A MAN WHO WANTS TO BE AN ASSET*, he claimed credit for bringing attention to an important problem. "The crime was tragic," he wrote, "but it did serve society, urging it to come to the aid of its members in distress or danger. . . . It is necessary to sometimes get involved." He said that his self-improvement campaign had enriched relations between inmates and guards at Attica and made him a new person. "The man who killed Kitty Genovese in Queens in 1964 is no more. I'm a man who wants to be an asset to society."

In 1979 Moseley concocted a new account of the murder. He had cut Kitty off in traffic, he now claimed. She had jumped out of her Fiat and shouted at him, calling him "nigger." So he snapped and killed her with a knife he happened to be carrying. Moseley went further: He said he deserved credit for "demonstrating restraint" during his rampage in Buffalo and Grand Island. Yes, he had raped Zella Moore and Janet Kulaga, but that as much as proved his point. "I could have killed them," he said.

Moseley reported to his first parole hearing at Green Haven, New York, on January 31, 1984. Still slender after nineteen and a half years in prison, not counting his four-day jailbreak, the forty-eight-year-old inmate sat in a conference room opposite three correction-department commissioners. According to confidential minutes of the hearing, the commissioners began with a synopsis of his record: murder in the first degree, death sentence commuted to twenty years to life, an escape featuring "rapes with dimensions of sadism," followed by sixteen relatively uneventful years behind bars. Perhaps he was a bit of a whiner, sending prison officials an eye-rolling volume of suggestions and complaints. He'd had a female "friend" who broke visitation rules by letting him paw her too intimately. These and other violations, called "tickets," had earned him a total of more than three years of solitary confinement. Even so he caused less trouble than many other inmates. "I wouldn't call you a model prisoner, but you are fairly close to it," commissioner Joseph Mulholland told him at the hearing, "certainly no big headache." Mulholland asked the prisoner if he had anything to say.

"I'm terribly sorry. Sort of ashamed, really," he said. Still he felt that those sixteen relatively headache-free years should tip the scales in his favor. In fact, he said, his twenty years of incarceration amounted to more suffering than crime victims endured, "because for a victim it's a one-time or one-hour or one-minute affair, but for the person who's caught, it's forever."

"Well, that's one way to look at it," a parole board commissioner noted.

"It's debatable that you're as bad off as Miss Genovese," said another. Moseley went on to make a better point by insisting that inmates need some hope of success to keep parole hearings from becoming a charade. Still the board denied his bid for limited freedom. He was denied again in 1986 and 1988. Since then he has appeared before the board every two years, fifteen times in all, with no hint that he will ever be paroled. His hearings have featured moments of regret, anger, and even low comedy. In 1986 a board member asked about the foreign object he stuck up his rectum at Attica. "Did you do that purposely?"

"Yes."

"What was the object?"

"To get to the hospital," Moseley said.

"I mean, what was the object that you inserted?"

"A can."

At his sixth parole hearing, in 1994, a fifty-eight-year-old Moseley sounded sick of his biennial letdowns. When a commissioner asked about his murderous impulses, he said, "I don't have those feelings anymore."

"How do we know that is true?"

He asked, "How do you know anything that anyone tells you is true?" The inmate went on to mock the commissioners' talk of rehabilitation, describing his time in prison as "thirty years of punishment, period! I come back in two years and still don't get paroled. I think you made your decision before I got here."

"You are entitled to your opinion," the commissioner said, noting Moseley's history of "very violent criminal behavior. Very heinous criminal behavior, whether it occurred thirty or fifty years ago. We have a right to be concerned about your behavior."

"I didn't say you don't. But you just made the point that it did occur thirty years ago."

"I said *whether* it occurred thirty or fifty years ago."

"So in other words you judge a person—"

"We are not here to answer questions, Mr. Moseley. You are."

"Are you finished? *You finished?*" With that the inmate stood and stalked out of the hearing room.

A year later Moseley filed a lawsuit demanding a new trial. His claim was that Sidney Sparrow, his trial lawyer in 1964, had a conflict of interest. A writer for the *New York Law Journal* reading the thirty-year-old trial transcript had run across Sparrow's odd announcement that he couldn't handle the case "objectively, calmly" because he had represented Kitty "for years."

Barry Rhodes agreed to handle Moseley's petition. During their conferences, attorney Rhodes says, "I found Moseley to be polite, articulate, intelligent. He was able to comprehend the legal permutations of his case, which is more than you can say for a lot of people in his position. A pleasant guy, for a serial murderer. We didn't discuss the details of the original crime, the necrophilia and oral sex with a woman who was menstruating, because I didn't need to vomit."

Rhodes recalls sitting in a prison library with his graying fifty-nine-year-old client when Rhodes noticed a cockroach on the floor. He tried to step on it, but the roach skittered away. "They've got a sixth sense. They know you're coming after them," he said.

"No," Moseley said. "They've got cilia, little hairs on their bodies. They can feel the air currents from your foot." Rhodes looked it up later; his client was right.

In court, Rhodes hinted darkly about links between Kitty and the Mafia. Her younger brother Vincent, now pushing sixty, was called to the witness stand to swear once again that their family had nothing to do with the Genovese crime family. In the end a federal judge denied Moseley's petition for a new trial, ruling that Sparrow had served his client well, and it turned out that Sparrow's blurting about representing Kitty "for years" had been misunderstood. When Judge Shapiro cut him off, Sparrow was trying to say *four* years: "I represented her four years ago." The court reporter had typed *for* for *four*. Sparrow had mentioned working with Kitty because he hoped the jurors would spare Moseley's life despite their sympathy for her, which he shared.

After the U.S. District Court in Brooklyn rejected his petition, Moseley returned to prison in handcuffs, per regulations dating back to his escape, and followed a guard to his cell. Today he is prisoner number 64A0102 at Clinton Correctional Facility, a 169-year-old super-maximum penitentiary in the state's snow-swept northeast corner. As of late 2013 no living inmate had served more time in New York's prison system.

...

In the end it wasn't Winston Moseley who had an impact on society. It was Kitty.

Most murder victims are soon forgotten outside a small circle of family and friends. Even notorious cases fade in time. Who remembers pretty Elma Sands, whose murder made inch-tall headlines for weeks in 1800, or sex-scandal preacher Edward Hall, shot through the head in mysterious circumstances in 1922 (and buried near Boss Tweed in Green-Wood Cemetery), or *Dungeons & Dragons* player Dallas Egbert III in 1980, or a hundred more who were once household names? Yet the world remembers Kitty Genovese. In his 1974 memoir, *Chief!*, Seedman remembered her as "a compact, dark-eyed and well shaped barmaid." The chief of detectives outed her too, revealing "a sensitive fact about Kitty Genovese: She was a lesbian." To Seedman that label justified the Queens detectives' harsh questioning of Mary Ann because gay lovers were known to be extra jealous. Confirming what tabloid readers may have gleaned from references to Kitty's "bohemian" lifestyle and "fast crowd," *Chief!* was a new affront to Kitty's survivors. Vincent Genovese had already followed his daughter into New Canaan's Lakeview Cemetery. Kitty's brothers and sister had spent years trying to shield their mother from news stories about the murder, but after Rachel died in 1993 they found a stack of clippings about the crime tucked into a desk drawer.

By then Bill Genovese had spent more than half his life in a wheelchair. Kitty's second-youngest brother joined the Marines in 1966 and served during the Vietnam War. "The question of apathy was with me in Vietnam," said Bill, who kept imagining how his sister had spent her last moments. In combat, "I became known for taking risks. I couldn't let anything go without trying to act." On March 13, 1967, the third anniversary of his sister's murder, twenty-year-old Bill stepped on a land mine. He lost both legs. Over the decades to come he kept tabs on a growing archive of news accounts, textbook studies, and other references to Kitty, whose name came up whenever someone died who might have been saved. One cultural reference was a violent, much-remembered short story by Harlan Ellison, "The Whimper of Whipped Dogs," in which New Yorkers watch a killer knife an innocent girl to death.

"The Kitty Genovese story hit me with the impact of a piledriver," Ellison recalls. "I made that story part of a collection, *Deathbird Stories*, about contemporary American gods: the gods of the slot machine, automobiles, and mass marketing. This was the god of the city streets. It was as if she were sacrificed by people attending a Black Mass."

On Christmas Day 1974 fashion model Sandra Zahler's boyfriend attacked her in her apartment in the Mowbray building overlooking Austin Street. A neighbor heard a crash, an angry voice, and Zahler's cries of "No, no!" No one knocked on her door or phoned 911 while Zahler was beaten to death. The neighbor told police that she thought the superintendent would call. Newspapers had another apathy story for the Genovese file.

That holiday season a cast of television veterans began filming the first screen treatment of Kitty's story. *Death Scream*, an ABC television movie, starred Raul Julia as a detective tracking a killer who stabs a young New York woman in full view of the neighbors in her apartment building. Diahann Carroll played a frantic drunken neighbor based on Karl Ross, while Edward Asner, Cloris Leachman, Kate Jackson, *Gilligan's Island*'s Tina Louise, and ten-year-old Helen Hunt played other witnesses ("witlesses" in one review). Art Carney and Nancy Walker stood in for the Koshkins, bickering over the phone. "What'll you tell them?" Carney asks his wife. "You heard a scream. 'Who screamed?' they'll ask. 'Who are you?' Always questions. They'll come up here and ask more questions. Anyway, the screens have stopped."

In 1984 the *Times* sent Maureen Dowd, thirty-two, to cover an event at Fordham University, the Catherine Genovese Memorial Conference on Bad Samaritanism. Dowd reported that Kitty's killing "occurred in a more innocent era, before the cynicism of Vietnam and Watergate and before national crime statistics began to mushroom. It crystallized what people were only beginning to feel about urban life in America: the anonymity, the lack of human contact, the feeling of not being able to control one's environment." She quoted sociologists, criminologists, cops, and U.S. surgeon general C. Everett Koop, whose keynote speech promised a better America "when people learn to care, when they accept the fact that there may be risks to caring, and when they agree to take those risks." Dowd also spoke to Dr. Harold Takooshian, the young Fordham professor with a more nuanced view. The crime was "complex," Takooshian said. "Some people were probably apathetic, but some were afraid of the killer. Some misinterpreted what was happening and thought it was a lovers' quarrel. Some might have wanted to get involved but didn't know what to do." Bernard Titowsky, who owned the Austin Book Shop, told Dowd that he had gone to work the next morning and found Kitty's blood on his doorstep. "Time and rain washed most of it away," he said.

Later in 1984 many New Yorkers cheered Kew Gardens–born subway vigilante Bernhard Goetz for shooting four young black men he claimed tried to mug him. Again the Genovese case became part of the discussion, as if crime victims—white crime victims, at least—were saying, *Never again*. According to Mayor Ed Koch, "Today the likelihood of a crowd averting its eyes is much less likely. Today we have to worry about vigilantism, the other extreme." In 1986–'87, the graphic novel *Watchmen* depicted an alternate America in which superheroes fought street crime after helping the United States win the Vietnam War. As the *Watchmen* saga opens, antihero Rorschach, working for a New York dressmaker, fashions a shape-shifting mask from charmed fabric—a dress Kitty Genovese ordered in the days before she died—and kills perps who have it coming. *Watchmen* would help inspire scattered bands of "real-life superheroes" who donned masks (and sometimes capes and tool belts) to moonlight as crime-stoppers. "Tonight, Golden Valkyrie and I are going out to honor the memory of not just Kitty Genovese, but of all those who have suffered because of the apathy of society," said a costumed crusader calling himself Silver Sentinel. It was easy to dismiss wannabes like him, who were sometimes pelted with pebbles and bottle caps. Many of their missions consisted of handing out sandwiches and water to homeless people or literally walking old ladies across streets, but they also broke up fights and foiled a few muggings and sexual assaults.

With crime rising as the 1990s approached, the *Times* marked the twenty-fifth anniversary of Kitty's murder by quoting the owner of Bailey's Pub: "No death that has come since can compare to it. That's where things changed—the beginning of the end of decency." It was a time when "Fun City" was seen as a theme park for muggers, rapists, and killers, a real-life prequel to John Carpenter's sci-fi film *Escape from New York*, in which a 400 percent jump in violent crime led the government to turn the city into a prison surrounded by fifty-foot walls. In fact, *Escape from New York* slightly understated the city's increase in violent crime. Homicides rose from 548 in the year before Kitty died to 2,245 in 1990, a jump of 410 percent. New York City was the homicide capital of America, accounting for a tenth of all murders nationwide.

In 1994, almost three decades after mayoral candidate John Lindsay delivered his anticrime speech in Kew Gardens, President

Bill Clinton made his own pilgrimage to the crime scene. The Kitty Genovese murder, said Clinton, "sent a chilling message about what had happened at that time in society, suggesting that we were each of us not simply in danger but fundamentally alone." Four years later, in the final episode of *Seinfeld*, Jerry, Elaine, George, and Kramer videotaped a carjacking for their own amusement and ended the series behind bars, jailed under a Good Samaritan law. A more solemn nod to the legacy of the Genovese case opened the 1999 action film *The Boondock Saints*. "I am reminded of the sad story of Kitty Genovese," says a priest in a holiday sermon. "A long time ago, this poor soul cried out for help time and time again. Though many saw, no one called the police. They all just watched as Kitty was stabbed to death in broad daylight. They watched her assailant walk away. Now, we must all fear evil men, but there is another kind of evil which we must fear most, and that is the indifference of good men." The *Boondock* homily was an incensed update of Edmund Burke's oft-quoted line, "All that is necessary for the triumph of evil is that good men do nothing." (Aptly enough in this context, Burke never said it.) Like most references to Kitty's story, the film scrambled the details while posing larger questions: How could we let Kitty die that way? What did her lonely dying mean?

Kitty Genovese's presence in the popular mind outlasted the century she lived in. Malcolm Gladwell's 2000 bestseller *The Tipping Point* repeated the *Times*' view of Kitty "attacked three times," though other sources had corrected the *Times*' error. There were two attacks, not three. Gladwell accepted the "fact" that "thirty-eight of her neighbors watched from their windows." He noted the conventional wisdom that "the alienation of big-city life makes people hard and unfeeling. The truth about Genovese, however, turns out to be a little more complicated—and more interesting." Gladwell went on to give his readers a lucid introduction to the bystander effect, but at the cost of promoting the myth of thirty-eight eyewitnesses.

Then, in the run-up to the United States' 2002 war in Iraq, President George W. Bush's defense advisor Paul Wolfowitz invoked the case to support an invasion. According to the *Times,* Wolfowitz "often talks about Kitty Genovese, the New York woman murdered in 1964 while dozens of neighbors watched from their apartment windows." When a deputy secretary of defense casts Winston Moseley as Saddam Hussein and Kitty as Iraq, the uses of her ordeal have gone too far.

19

Case Studies

On a Friday evening in February 2013, forty students drifted into an eighth-floor classroom on Fordham University's campus on Manhattan's Upper West Side. They brought backpacks, textbooks, laptops, Beats by Dr. Dre headphones, carrot sticks and Sun Chips to munch, Starbucks coffee and Red Bull to combat the night-class blahs. The subject was urban psychology. The professor was Harold Takooshian, the world's foremost academic authority on the Kitty Genovese case.

A shy, sturdy man with a shock of black hair and a thin caterpillar mustache, the sixty-one-year-old professor dresses up for class. While his students wore T-shirts, hoodies, and jeans, he sported a navy blazer, crisp white shirt, and red bow tie. A bell rang—the same sort of old-fashioned school bell that rings in Winston Moseley's cell block every morning at seven—and Takooshian carried a full-page photo to the whiteboard behind the teacher's desk: the 1961 mug shot of Kitty in her dark checked blouse. One of the male students said she looked kind of hot.

"This is a special class," Takooshian said, taping the photo to the whiteboard a little above eye level, a tradition of his. He likes people to look Kitty in the eye when they talk about her. "Let's have a show of hands—how many of you are familiar with the 1964 murder of Kitty Genovese?" He asks his undergrads that question each year, and year after year more than half his students raise their hands. That evening it was twenty-three out of forty. They were far too young to remember the story as news. Some had parents who were born after the crime. They knew the case from previous psych and sociology classes. Takooshian's role, as he saw it, was to pull Kitty out of their textbooks, to help them see the case as something that happened to a real person and to see her as more than an answer on next week's exam. It was a role he took seriously, not as a job but as a vocation in the best sense.

"People have been talking and thinking about this case for a long time, but we haven't completely figured it out," he said. "I don't want to use the wrong word, but I think it's something holy."

Over the next two hours he asked his class to look at the case and its subsequent history from multiple vantage points. For starters, he asked whether people should be required by law to help their fellow citizens.

"How would that work?" asked a student in a Knicks cap. "Say you help a person with a broken neck."

"Yes, you could make it worse," Takooshian said.

"And then you're screwed—they'd sue you for millions." That was an issue Phil Ochs anticipated in 1967. In the song inspired by Kitty's murder, Ochs pictured witnesses ignoring the victims of a thirteen-car pileup: *we gotta move and we might get sued.*

"Maybe the law should protect concerned citizens from lawsuits. If you intervene in good faith, you couldn't get sued," Takooshian said. In fact all fifty states now had Good Samaritan laws of one kind or another. New York's was typical: no one was expected to endanger himself, but if a doctor stopped to help an accident victim, for example, he couldn't be sued as long as he acted reasonably.

A young woman sucking a lollipop raised her hand. "What if there's a wreck in the middle of the highway? You could cause more accidents running out to help."

"That's a good point. But isn't apathy worse? What if I laugh at a rapist holding a woman at knifepoint?"

"That makes you a jerk, not a criminal."

"The minimum should be calling the police," someone said.

Most New Yorkers agree with that. A recent poll found that 82 percent believe that the law should require citizens to act—to phone 911 at least—in what Takooshian called a "Genovese-type" situation. "And it's easy these days. Forty or fifty years ago you needed a phone booth." That line got a laugh from his students; he may as well have said "smoke signals." Of course the 911 system was no panacea, Takooshian said, particularly in New York. America's largest, busiest emergency-response program was perhaps its worst, plagued by dropped calls and delays. (The failures of New York's 911 system made headlines later in 2013.) He also enjoyed shooting holes in his students' TV-based ideas of police efficiency. "What would happen if a real cop shot the lock off a door? He'd castrate himself!" Real police work was tedious. Real police work was usually ineffective. "How many street crimes result in an arrest? Two percent." Concerned citizens might do better, he said, if they tried.

Takooshian practiced what he professed. He was thought to be the only Fordham professor to make a citizen's arrest, a distinction he earned when he and two friends foiled a 1981 smash-and-grab car theft, wrestling a crowbar-wielding burglar to the curb and holding him until a policeman took over. Takooshian had lived through the *Death Wish* days and nights of rampant street crime in New York. One night he was climbing onto his motorcycle when two punks jumped him. One got him in a headlock; the other waved a knife. Struggling, he heard the first one say, "Give me the knife, I want to stab him!" The young professor looked up to see several well-dressed pedestrians watching as if his plight were mildly interesting. Feeling a surge of what he calls bystander rage, he fought off the punks, who ran while Takooshian yelled at the bystanders: "You wanted to see me get *stabbed*, didn't you?"

Thirty years later he told his class, "We started this class in 1984, a time when punks outside this building would break into our students' cars. The city is safer now." In some small but significant part, he believed, the city was safer thanks to the legacy of the Genovese case.

He recalled the stunts he and his students staged in the pre-liability heyday of social-science experiments. They had an actress place a pile of fur coats into a car, which was promptly broken into by a "thug" with a crowbar. Three hundred fake thefts later, only eighteen bystanders had taken action of any sort. His students also staged a kidnapping. "We actually abducted someone on the street. Most people did nothing. They didn't want to get involved." But that was back in the '80s. No social-psychology professor could direct that sort of street theater in 2013. If Takooshian wanted to continue exploring what Kitty's dying meant, he needed a new way to do it.

There were mysteries here, even fifty years later. Wrapping up his lecture while her mug shot loomed over his shoulder, Takooshian asked questions: Why did so many people still remember her? How much of her legacy had to do with the apathy of her neighbors? How much had to do with the picture hanging over his shoulder? What if Kitty hadn't been so good-looking, with a sort of charisma that still seems to comes off that photo? Would we mourn her the same way if she had been black, or old, or overweight? Would anyone remember her name?

Over his thirty years of studying the Kitty Genovese case, teaching it at Fordham, and organizing conferences devoted to it, Takooshian hoped to turn up some undiscovered fact about her murder, something to suggest that the half hour of her death was anything but lonely torture. Some moment of mercy, however brief, would be a favor to her memory. As it was, he reminded his class that her suffering wasn't meaningless. While the reforms that followed her murder came too late to be any consolation to her, they had saved other lives. That was part of what he meant when he said there was something holy about her story. "The hour of her death has been microscopically analyzed by criminal investigators, journalists, and psychologists," says Takooshian. "It was an hour not of her own choosing, when she suddenly found herself excruciatingly alone. Her screams may have been ignored by her neighbors at the time, but they have been heard around the world and touched millions of people since then."

Twenty years after organizing the Catherine Genovese Memorial Conference that Maureen Dowd covered in 1984, Takooshian chaired another Memorial Conference to mark the crime's fortieth anniversary. He opened the proceedings by saying that society owes Kitty a debt. Her murder "brought a problem to our attention, a problem now known as Genovese Syndrome." He noted the odd fact that her contribution, tragic and unwilling as it was, is almost unique—"Who else is known for the last thirty minutes of their life?" He also praised Abraham Rosenthal for spurring interest with his book, *Thirty-Eight Witnesses*. "It is hard to think of a non-science book that has had more impact on the behavioral sciences. Rosenthal's bold challenge spawned new specialties in psychology."

Curtis Sliwa, adjusting his red beret, followed Takooshian to the podium. Sliwa recalled seeing Kitty's name in the papers—"I was nine years old"—and said her murder had inspired him to found the Guardian Angels, a volunteer corps of more than four thousand crime-fighters who now patrolled streets in 144 cities. Sliwa recalled "a malaise gripping the city after the murder. Many people were ready to fly the white flag." Proclaiming that citizens, not policemen, are the first line of defense against crime, he urged every citizen to honor Kitty's memory by helping others. "If we dare to care," he said, "people won't put windowsills on their eyes, cotton balls in their ears, and zippers on their mouths, and these tragedies won't occur."

Journalist Jim Rasenberger spoke about discrepancies between the *Times*' famed front-page story and facts that emerged later. Like John Melia of the *Daily News*, who raised questions about the *Times*' reporting in a 1984 column, Rasenberger was a Genovese skeptic. He believed that the popular view of the murder, the *Times*' version that embarrassed Kew Gardens and symbolized the city's plunge into darkness—the version retold in *The Tipping Point* and countless psychology textbooks—was just this side of fiction. Rasenberger didn't relish delivering this news to a few dozen students, professors, and concerned citizens at Fordham that night. "The irony, of course," he said, "is that if the story had not been exaggerated it would have been a three-day story, maybe a five-day story, and we would not be here today, talking about it."

Later, Takooshian opened the floor to comments from the audience. There was the usual lull of self-conscious coughs. Then a portly senior citizen came forward. Nattily dressed in a gray suit, a scarf, a crisp white shirt, and purple bow tie, squinting through oversized glasses, Abraham Rosenthal took the floor as if the floor belonged to him. He was eighty-one years old. Long retired from the *Times*, the Pulitzer Prize–winning writer and editor was at Fordham to set the record straight.

Rosenthal told a rapt audience about his long-ago lunch with police commissioner Murphy. "He asked me, 'Have you heard about the story in Queens? You gave it one paragraph,'" he said, recalling the *Times*' brief second-day mention of the murder, two weeks before Gansberg's front-page story. "It was true. One paragraph. I couldn't rest with one paragraph."

The second-day story had actually been four paragraphs long. But Rosenthal hadn't come to the Genovese Memorial Conference on a rainy night to count paragraphs. This was the man whose passion for Kitty's plight had made her name famous and kept it alive for decades. His heart was in the right place even if that was a place where the facts don't get in the way of a good story. Rosenthal wanted to defend his paper's reporting down to the precise number of witnesses.

"Thirty-eight," he said, looking over his shoulder at Rasenberger. "Yes, thirty-eight! I never said, nor did anybody at the *New York Times*, that there were thirty-eight peering out a window. It was a *total* of thirty-eight, and we took the intelligence of the reader to understand that." Listeners looked puzzled, but Rosenthal paid them no mind. He had more to say. A story to tell.

"I grew up with five sisters, all older," he said, "and one of my sisters was murdered. My eldest sister, Bess. A delicious girl, absolutely delicious." Bess was coming home alone one evening through a desolate part of the city when a man surprised her. "A man, a pervert, jumped out of the bushes and killed her!" Rosenthal was shouting now. "She *was* Catherine Genovese. And she was my sister. This is the first time in my life that I've said so."

He took a breath. Fighting tears, he said the pervert "exposed himself to Bess. She ran and she ran and she ran! She had to run about a mile, and by the time she got home she was in a sweat. And she caught a cold. There were no drugs to speak of in those days, and two days later, she died. And I believe that he was guilty of murder. I don't care whether she was murdered technically—this person took her life away! Just as the monster who killed Catherine Genovese killed her."

Rosenthal stood with his fist clenched as if he were ready to fight, but there was only applause.

20

Revisions

And then there was Joseph De May, defender of the neigh-borhood.

"Kitty felt safe, even at three in the morning," he says, "and why wouldn't she? Kew Gardens was virtually crime-free."

De May became fascinated with the case after moving to Kew Gardens. An attorney who commuted to a Manhattan office from the Long Island Rail Road station, he passed the crime scene every day. The block was and still is almost unchanged since the night Kitty died—the chipped sidewalk, the oaks and sycamores rising from dirt squares in the sidewalk, some of the same storefronts facing the Mowbray building across Austin Street. The Ascend Day Spa now occupies the corner where the pharmacy used to be, but several other shops Kitty knew are still there. The Interlude Coffee House became an Internet café.

"The Mowbray dates back to the 1920s," De May says. "These trees were planted in the 1910s." Stepping past the eighteen-space railroad-station parking lot, he points to the sidewalk where Kitty ran from Moseley. "And this is where she was attacked and screamed bloody murder." De May, sixty-four, has a high forehead, thinning hair, and an aquiline nose with a tilt that suits his penchant for sniffing out facts others may have missed. As a maritime lawyer he has spent four decades immersed in freight rates, salvage rights, wake damage, and even piracy insurance. In his spare time he delved into the crime that made his neighborhood notorious, "and the more time I spent with it, the more questions I had."

He has studied the *Times'* front-page story of March 27, 1964, dozens of times as if it were a legal brief. Comparing the story to police reports, trial transcripts, and other news accounts, "I found six factual errors in the first paragraph." Here is how De May might annotate that paragraph:

For more than half an hour [no witnesses saw the crime for nearly that long], *38 respectable, law-abiding citizens in Queens* [but no more than two who clearly knew what was happening] *watched a killer stalk and stab a woman in three* [two] *separate attacks in Kew Gardens. Twice* [Once] *the sound of their voices and the sudden glow of their bedroom lights interrupted him and frightened him off. Each time he returned, sought her out and stabbed her again. Not one person telephoned the police during the assault* [probably false]; *one witness called after the woman was dead* [Kitty was still alive].

De May came to believe that editor Rosenthal tacked that paragraph on top of Gansberg's story. "And of course that's the paragraph people remembered."

Soon after he moved to the area in 1974, De May joined the Kew

Gardens Civic Association and the local historical society. Comparing notes with longtime residents, he found that many recalled the days when local families left their doors unlocked at night. Like him, they were worldly enough and proud enough of their village of fifteen thousand citizens to compare the arched Lefferts Boulevard Bridge over the L.I.R.R. tracks to the Ponte Vecchio in Florence. Many old-timers were annoyed that outsiders tended to know Kew Gardens only as the site of Kitty's murder, the place where "all those people watched that girl die." De May launched his own investigation, retracing Kitty's steps, knocking on doors, asking questions. Some of his neighbors confirmed what they had told Martin Gansberg years before. Some added a detail or two. Others wrote to the civic association's website, kewgardenshistory.com, which was soon devoted largely to the Genovese case. One former Kew Gardens resident told of hearing screams from the sidewalk on the first few anniversaries of Kitty's death. The screamer may have wanted to commemorate the crime, rebuke the neighbors, or both. After a few years the March 13 screams stopped. Another website visitor recalled that his family had moved into Karl Ross's old apartment in the late 1960s. The apartment at the top of the stairs had stood empty until the landlord cut the rent to a hundred dollars a month. "I endured some taunting from other kids over Kitty's ghost. Walking down the narrow stairway I sometimes thought of her, of her final moments and her whole future slipping away."

Another visitor to kewgardenshistory.com told De May he knew for a fact that the *Times*' account was wrong. He knew that at least one neighbor—his father—phoned the police that night. De May had found a witness Martin Gansberg, the police, and everyone else had missed. Michael Hoffman was fourteen in March 1964. His bedroom on the second floor of the Mowbray Apartments overlooked Austin Street. Around three o'clock in the morning on March 13, he was awakened by shouts from the street. He went to the window. The streetlamps over the sidewalk cast enough dim yellowish light for young Michael to see a man bent over a woman. "I heard what I thought was crying or moaning, a female voice. That's when my dad came into my room."

In 2003, Michael Hoffman, then fifty-four and living in Florida, gave a sworn statement detailing his memory of the assault. "My father asked me what was happening," he recalled. "I said, 'This guy just beat up a lady and ran away!'" From Michael's window they watched Kitty stagger around the corner drugstore, out of sight. "The way she walked made us think she was either drunk or had been beaten up. Dad decided to call the police in case she was hurt badly." Samuel Hoffman dialed "0" and asked the operator to connect him to the police. The operator put him on hold. Three or four minutes later a police dispatcher took the call. "A lady got beat up and was staggering around," Sam Hoffman said, "by the drugstore at the L.I.R.R. station." He gave the dispatcher his name, phone number, and address.

Then it was over. The sidewalk was empty. "I'm tired," Sam Hoffman said. He returned to his bedroom, leaving Michael standing by his window, waiting for something else to happen. Nothing did. Kitty was behind the building now, invisible to anyone watching from an Austin Street window. Michael climbed back into bed. "I propped my pillow up so I could see out the window. That's the last I remember. Dad woke me later that morning."

In the morning the block was swarming with cops. Detectives interviewed witnesses—the Koshkins, the Farrars, Robert Mozer, Andrée Picq, Karl Ross, and others—while teenagers Billy Corrado and Mike Farrar gaped at traces of blood on the sidewalk. The police took statements from Sam and Mike Hoffman but told them they probably wouldn't be needed because they hadn't seen much. "I remember my dad telling the police that if they had come when we called, she'd probably still be alive. For that he got a dirty look from the detective," Hoffman recalled in his 2003 affidavit. Lest anyone think he was anti-police, he mentioned his employment history. "I am a retired New York City police lieutenant."

Hoffman's sworn statement was one blow to the myth of thirty-eight silent witnesses. Reappraisals by Melia in the *Daily News*, Rasenberger in the *Times*, and De May on his website, as well as blogs and other sites, chipped away at the *Times*' iconic account. The online journal *Space and Culture* published an "urban physiognomy" dissecting the crime from a spatial standpoint, showing that no one—with the possible exception of Ross—could have seen both of Moseley's attacks on Kitty. By the time De May spoke at the fortieth-anniversary Catherine Genovese Memorial Conference in 2004, anyone willing to do a little Googling might have suspected that "thirty-eight witnesses" carried a whiff of urban legend. Still, like the legendary alligators in the city's sewers, the story survived. Of the ten most popular social-psychology textbooks of 2005, all carried accounts of the Genovese case, with all ten accounts maintaining that thirty-eight witnesses watched Kitty die without lifting a finger to help.

I n 2007 Rachel Manning, a British psychology professor with a nose ring and a piercing gaze, attacked the legend in *American Psychologist*. Along with her colleagues Mark Levine and Alan Collins, Manning described the Genovese case as "one of the most powerful and influential moments in the history of social psychology." The accepted view of the case, she wrote, had done more than frighten people in the 1960s, galvanize neighborhood watch groups, bring calls for an emergency phone system, and achieve pop-cultural status in books, films, and on the Web. "We suggest that, almost from its inception, the story of the thirty-eight witnesses became a kind of modern parable, the antonym of the parable of the Good Samaritan."

Manning and her coauthors saw the parable's persistence as a case of academic apathy. It was simply easier to promote Rosenthal's vivid picture of the crime, which commanded the attention of the press, police, public, and generations of college students, than to puzzle over the shards of a messier reality. Manning cited a typical textbook account: "Several years ago, a young woman named Kitty Genovese was stabbed to death in New York City. . . . [N]o fewer than thirty-eight of her neighbors came to their windows at three a.m. in response to her screams of terror—and remained at their windows in fascination for the thirty minutes it took her assailant to complete his grisly deed." Manning picked that description apart, leaving little intact but Kitty's and the city's names. Her analysis wasn't perfect. She mentioned trial witness Robert Mozer, who had shouted, "Leave that girl alone," to support her claim that prosecutors had called "witnesses with the best and most complete views." In fact, prosecutor Cacciatore's team had kept Karl Ross and Joseph Fink off the witness stand. Cacciatore didn't need them. He had Moseley's confession. He had the murder weapon. He chose to keep the jury focused on Moseley, and the jury's death sentence vindicated his choice, though it also kept the jury and eventually the world from distinguishing Ross and Fink from the rest of the nameless thirty-eight.

What explains the myth's staying power? One of its attractions was that it turned a facet of social psychology upside down. Everyone knew that mobs sometimes turned violent. Studies of the "madness of crowds" dated to the nineteenth century. Now it seemed that crowds could be a passive threat as well as an active one. While a rabid mob might tear someone limb from limb, a different crowd might stand by while an innocent person died. Manning also noted that textbook writers "are motivated to reduce complexity, keeping the story simple in an attempt to engage undergraduates." They often rely on secondary sources—usually other textbooks—without checking facts. Quoting Franz Samelson, she and her coauthors called "origin myths" like the Genovese story "a byproduct of pedagogy" serving to illustrate basic concepts and attract students. For the fields of social psychology and prosocial behavior, then, the Kitty Genovese case was like the apple that never really fell on Isaac Newton's head.

Manning, Levine, and Collins acknowledged the "historic role" the Genovese case had played. They weren't denying that the bystander effect exists. What disturbed them was that half a century's research was built around "a stubborn and intractable myth."

De May helped Manning and her colleagues research their *American Psychologist* article. They hoped to debunk their field's most persistent myth; he wanted to restore his town's good name.

"I understand why people believe the story of thirty-eight witnesses," De May said on one of his walks past the crime scene. He pointed out Fairchild Fine Furniture, now manned by a gray-haired Billy Corrado, the teenager who thought Kitty was so pretty when he helped his father move her sofa-bed upstairs. A few doors down, Bailey's Pub looked the same, though its sign read AUSTIN'S ALE HOUSE. The pub still stayed open until 4:00 a.m. most days. The old fifty-cent Rheingolds were now five-dollar Guinnesses. Across the street the hundred-foot-tall Mowbray still cast a long shadow almost a century after its heyday of debutante balls and new "ice-free iceboxes."

There was a barbershop at the corner of Austin and Lefferts, across from the still-ignored police callbox. There was a bodega selling newspapers, cigarettes, and lottery tickets. There was a second-run movie house, two pizza joints, and a fish market where pretty good sushi cost half what it sold for in Manhattan. De May led the way to the Village Diner, known for its pita wraps and Belgian waffles. "I'm an egg cream man myself," said the lifelong New Yorker. But the fizzy egg creams of his youth, made with milk, seltzer, and U-Bet chocolate syrup—no egg, no cream—were now harder to find than sushi. He settled for coffee.

De May had spent forty years trying to understand the Genovese case. He empathized with everyone from Kitty and Mary Ann to the harried detectives investigating the murder, *Times*men Gansberg and Rosenthal, and a 1960s public still reeling from the shock of the Kennedy assassination. He believed that the murders of John Kennedy and Kitty Genovese were linked. "The assassination was a tremendous blow to America. There was a school of thought that we all killed President Kennedy," he said. "What was wrong with us? Then, four months later, Kitty Genovese is killed while her neighbors watch. Why?" In his view, *why* is complicated.

"I'm not suggesting that anybody in Kew Gardens earned a good-citizenship medal that night. I'm saying that I believe the accepted story of the Genovese case has done a disservice to Kew Gardens. What happened to Kitty, tragic as it was, could have happened anywhere." The tragedy, then, was not where but how she died: terrified, helpless, and alone. "And most people who think they know what really happened, don't."

One thing they don't know is how Kitty's story ended. They don't know that she didn't die alone.

21

Thirty-Three Minutes

Kitty helped Victor Horan behind the bar at Ev's 11th Hour on Thursday night, the twelfth of March, 1964, serving shots and beers to the usual crowd. The regulars' choice was Jack Daniel's with a Rheingold back. Wilted newspapers on the bar carried ads for the week's new movie, *Becket*, with Richard Burton and Peter O'Toole, plus the holdovers *Dr. Strangelove* and *Captain Newman, M.D.* The sports pages previewed the defending American League champion Yankees and Stengel's sure-to-stink Mets, opening their third season next month at brand-new Shea Stadium. The ballpark wasn't even painted yet.

When the crowd thinned, Kitty went out for a drink with one of the regulars, a dockworker who hung out at Ev's. "Jack Timmins was his name," recalls Horan. "It was a bite to eat and a drink, not what you'd call a date—just Kitty being sociable." The paunchy, balding Timmins didn't look like someone you would expect to see dining with Kitty, who looked typically spruce in her gray flannel skirt and turquoise blouse, but she didn't mind. Kitty liked everybody. According to Timmins she had "about three drinks" that night.

The place was almost empty when she got back to Ev's. She told Horan he could close up a little early. At about 3:00 a.m., she picked up her suede jacket and left the bar.

"Goodnight, Vic," she said.

"'Night, Kitty."

Outside, her breath fogged the air. Clumps of dirty snow dotted both sides of wide Jamaica Avenue. Her cherry-red Fiat shivered when she started the engine. If she had closed the bar half an hour earlier or worked for another ten minutes, or even another minute, everything would have been different. If a stoplight had changed from green to red a block away, the white Corvair coming down Jamaica Avenue might have passed a minute later, after she drove away. Instead the Corvair did a U-turn and followed the Fiat.

There was hardly any traffic. She took the ramp onto Grand Central Parkway and sped west, shifting into fourth gear. There was a shorter route, Jamaica Avenue to Hillside Avenue to Kew Gardens Road, but Kitty enjoyed the sprint home. The Corvair had to speed up to stay close. Kitty took the Union Turnpike exit to Kew Gardens. From there it was three turns to Austin Street.

Finding no parking spaces on Austin, she parked in the Long Island Rail Road lot. It was 3:15 a.m. The Corvair idled at a bus stop thirty yards away. Kitty stepped out of the Fiat and spent a few seconds locking the driver's door. She loved her sporty little car.

Looking toward the Tudor building where she and Mary Ann lived, she saw a deserted block of Austin Street between the train station and Lefferts Boulevard. The Farrars were asleep. Mary Ann was asleep. The milkman and newspaper delivery trucks wouldn't start their morning rounds for at least another hour. Pale, pre-Lindsay streetlamps cast a pallid glow on the sidewalk, pools of yellow light muddied by the shadows of tree branches. The two-story Tudor building faced the hulking nine-story Mowbray, with its ranks of dark windows, on the other side of empty Austin Street.

Kitty stepped from the L.I.R.R. lot to the curb in front of Franken's Pharmacy. Now she heard something. Footsteps. She was about a hundred paces from the door that led to her apartment, but she went the other way, past the drugstore and Corrado's furniture shop, toward Lefferts Boulevard. There was a police callbox at the corner of Austin and Lefferts, but Kitty was probably thinking of Bailey's Pub on the same corner. There might still be people there. But luck was against her. Bailey's had a new bartender, a rookie who closed up before midnight when a fight broke out. Three and a half hours later the corner was quiet, storefronts dark. The footsteps she heard were coming closer.

Kitty began to run, but the man was faster. He jumped onto her. He drove her to the sidewalk and stabbed her in the back, right through her coat. Once, twice. Kitty screamed. At least once the blade of Moseley's serrated hunting knife cut deep enough to puncture one of her lungs. Still her voice reached a pitch that woke some of her neighbors. She screamed again, then somehow she found the presence of mind to call out in words. "Oh God," she cried, "I've been stabbed."

Lights popped on in windows overlooking the street. It was 3:20. The rest of the night's chronology may vary by a minute or two, but one witness checked her bedside clock at that instant, about a minute after the attack began. It read 3:20. Neighbors on both sides of the street heard Kitty cry for help. She shouted, "Oh God he stabbed me. Help me!" She may have said, "Help me, I'm dying." But most witnesses heard indistinct screams. It was late, they were groggy. By the time they got to their windows she was on her knees struggling to stand up. Moseley stood over her with his knife in his hand.

On the seventh floor of the Mowbray, Robert Mozer lifted his window, one hundred and ten feet from where Kitty knelt. "Leave that girl alone!" Mozer yelled.

Moseley looked up.

In her fourth-floor Mowbray apartment, stewardess Andrée Picq heard Mozer shout and went to her window. Sam and Marjorie Koshkin went to their window in the West Virginia Apartments. On the Mowbray's second floor, Irene Frost heard a shriek. Down the hall from Frost, fourteen-year-old Mike Hoffman woke up. Another Mowbray dweller, Madeline Hartmann, heard screams. None of them had seen the stabbing. Joseph Fink, the Mowbray's assistant superintendent, was the only one with a clear view. Fink watched for several minutes, standing in front of the brass elevator in the lobby, before he took the elevator to the basement to take a nap.

Karl Ross heard a commotion outside his window in the Tudor building. Ross was drunk; he ignored it. Sophie and Joe Farrar's bedroom was a few windows down from Ross's; Kitty's screams woke Sophie, but by the time she got to her window the street was quiet again. Sophie went back to sleep.

Moseley remembered his Corvair, sitting right there where anybody could see it. He hurried off to move it, leaving Kitty kneeling in front of the Austin Book Shop. Irene Frost, looking out her window, saw Moseley hurry toward the bus stop. Sam Koshkin went to a side window and saw Moseley back his car into the shadows.

Kitty was getting to her feet. She was not mortally wounded. She would live if she got help now. Bracing herself on the Tudor building, she stepped toward Franken's Pharmacy. With a hand on the drugstore window, moving as if she were sleepwalking, she went around Franken's, past the spot where she had parked her car. Fink, Frost, Mike Hoffman and his father, the Koshkins, and a few others saw her. Had she screamed now—who knows?—they might have run downstairs. Had she fallen in front of the drugstore they might have called the police. But she walked without making a sound. She must have been in shock. Her lungs were collapsing. To Marjorie Koshkin her unsteady walk seemed to take "an eternity." Had Kitty struggled to her feet and walked the other way, toward Bailey's, everyone on the block could have seen her. Someone might have helped. Instead she went around the drugstore, turning left, away from Austin Street toward the railroad tracks and the dark in back of her building. Toward home. She was trying to reach the door that led to her apartment, where Mary Ann slept. And the moment she went around the corner drugstore, everyone looking through an Austin Street window lost sight of her. Anyone who was thinking of phoning the police had reason to hesitate. What was there to report? A woman yelled, an empty street. Andrée Picq dialed her phone, panicked, and hung up. Sam Koshkin reached for his phone, but his wife said no. "They must have had thirty calls." Fourteen-year-old Mike Hoffman, standing at his bedroom window, heard his father telling a police dispatcher, "A lady got beat up. . . ."

Kitty staggered past the dark, locked Interlude Coffee House. Twenty steps from the street-level door that led to her apartment, she must have realized she lacked the strength to walk that far. The door marked 82-62 was closer. The door that led upstairs to Karl Ross's apartment. She pushed through the outside door to the vestibule and collapsed at the foot of the stairs. It must have been a relief to get inside. It was warm in here. Whoever stabbed her was gone. She could rest. She could wait for help. Did she think, lying in the vestibule at 82-62 Austin Street, that there was something familiar about these narrow stairs under a single lightbulb? They were almost a match for the stairs in the Brooklyn brownstone where she grew up.

Moseley sat in his car in the dark a hundred yards away, quizzing himself. Drive home? Give it up? What if the shouting man called the police? What if somebody else did? Was it crazy to go after the white girl again, and what if it was? He didn't hear any police sirens. The shouting man across the street wasn't leading a posse down to the sidewalk. Nobody was going to help the white girl. Moseley tossed his stocking cap aside and put on the fedora with a feather in the brim. Jaunty as an alpine hiker he ambled to the waiting room at the rail station. Was she hiding there? No. He tried the coffeehouse. Locked. From there it was ten paces to a door marked 82-62. Unlocked. Inside he found Kitty.

We can only imagine her terror at seeing the monster again. Despite punctured lungs she called out loud enough to rouse Karl Ross from his stupor. To Ross's consternation the noise was coming from the other direction! The shouts he'd heard from the sidewalk outside his window were coming from the vestibule outside his front door.

With the last of her strength Kitty cried out again. That made Moseley mad. He *had* to finish what he'd started. He kept trying to hold her down and stab her at the same time, trying to kill her so that he could then rape her, but she kept squirming, fighting, making too much noise. He stabbed her in the larynx. Kitty could only moan after that. Moseley stabbed her stomach. He stabbed her breast deep enough to cut through two of her ribs. Still she fought. At one point she grabbed the knife's blade. She twisted and turned. Moseley lost count of how many times he stabbed before she was quiet enough for him to hear the door creak at the top of the stairs.

Ross peeked out from behind his door. He saw Moseley on top of Kitty Genovese, bloody knife in his hand. Moseley looked up. Ross slapped his door shut. He was afraid. Drunk and afraid. He peeked out again. It was still happening.

It was between 3:40 and 3:45 A.M. Moseley raised the knife. Kitty was still trying to fight him off. The details of what happened in the next few minutes—Mosley's sexual assault—would appear in the coroner's report, detectives' and lawyers' notes, and courtroom transcripts. Those grisly details would loom over movies and TV programs, true-crime stories, novels and blog posts devoted to the case, complicating attempts to remember the victim as more than a victim. But Kitty was a lively young woman full of hopes for her future, deserving dignity and more life. With that person in mind, this is the time to avert one's eyes.

Finally Ross phoned a friend. "Don't get involved," the friend said. Head pounding, the dog groomer tried to think straight. He phoned a neighbor, Carol Tarantino. "Come over," she told him.

But Ross couldn't use his door, not with the killer out there. He climbed out his window and began crawling across the roof.

Moseley was finished. Pocketing his knife, he went through Kitty's blood- and semen-stained clothing. He took the billfold with forty-nine dollars inside. Just being practical. He stood up and dusted himself off. Kitty was still breathing.

Carol Tarantino phoned another neighbor, Greta Schwartz. Somebody was stabbing Kitty Genovese! Where? The stairs—outside Karl Ross's door! What should they do?

Schwartz called the Farrars' apartment. Sophie Farrar said, "Call the police!" She grabbed a coat and ran for the door.

Ross finally phoned the police. A TS officer logged the call at 3:55 but must not have been paying close attention because Patrolman Clarence Kron, assigned to the 102nd Precinct, received a radio dispatch at 3:50: *AMBULANCE NEEDED AT 82-62 AUSTIN STREET.*

Thirteen-year-old Mike Farrar ran to the kitchen in his pajamas. "What's going on?" He saw his father hopping on one foot, trying to get his pants on in time to follow his wife downstairs. "It's okay," Joe Farrar said. "Go back to bed."

Mike's mother, all four feet and eleven inches of her, was out the door. Sophie ran downstairs to the doorway in back of the building, facing the train tracks. It was dark back there. Dark and cold, thirty-four degrees. It was fifty steps from the Farrars' apartment to the door marked 82-62, the door that led to Ross's apartment.

For all Sophie knew she was running straight into a murder in progress. All she knew was that somebody was attacking Kitty Genovese. Whoever it was might want to give her the same treatment. Sophie could have waited for the police. She could at least have waited for her husband to catch up. Instead she ran down the stairs.

It was cold out. Sophie ran for the door under the awning at 82-62. Inside, Kitty lay on the floor like a rag doll under the naked bulb in the ceiling. Her clothes were torn, skin and underwear exposed. Sophie knelt and put her arms around her. Kitty reacted. She flailed blindly, still trying to fend off the knife. Sophie reached for her hand. That was when she noticed the blood. There was blood on Kitty's shoes and on the walls. "She was moaning," Sophie remembers, "going uh-uh-uh." Sophie hugged her and spoke to her.

"Kitty, it's Sophie. Shh, it's okay. It's Sophie, it's okay, I'm here. . . ."

Sophie looked up to see Karl Ross at the top of the stairs. He must have slipped back into his apartment. She said, "Give me a towel. She's bleeding." Ross ducked into his apartment for a hand towel, but couldn't bring himself to approach the bloody scene. Gently as she could, Sophie rested Kitty's head on the floor. She hurried up the stairs, took the towel, returned to her side.

At 3:52, thirty-three minutes after the first attack, Patrolman Kron pulled up outside Franken's Pharmacy. He parked a few feet from Kitty's Fiat. Kron stepped out of his squad car. Someone shouted from a second-floor window, "Around the back, around the back!" As Kron reported later, he hurried past the pharmacy and the Interlude Coffee House to the next door down, where he found a young woman in an older woman's arms, "with blood around the lower parts of her body."

Sophie kept talking, saying, "It's okay, they're coming. It won't be long." She could tell that Kitty heard her because she stopped struggling. Kitty was still trying to breathe, but some of the tension went out of her. Sophie said, "Kitty, shh. You'll be okay. They're coming, they're coming. Help's coming."

Acknowledgments

This book would have been far shorter and less comprehensive without the contributions of three people who care deeply about Kitty Genovese and her story.

Mary Ann Zielonko, who prizes her privacy and still mourns the partner she lost half a century ago, spent hours with me on the phone and in a New England coffee shop, sharing memories she had kept to herself since 1964. I owe Mary Ann my heartfelt thanks as well as a lifetime subscription to the *Village Voice*.

Janine Abel of the Queens County District Attorney's Office, who has visited Kitty's grave to pay her respects while working to keep Winston Moseley in prison, shared a crucial discovery with me: a trove of long-lost documents that made *Kitty Genovese* far more comprehensive than it could have been without her help. The hard-working, heroic Ms. Abel deserves a vote of thanks from anyone who finds the book worth reading.

Professor Harold Takooshian of Fordham University has honored Kitty's memory for thirty years. "Takoosh" was my Virgil during more than a year of researching the academic side of the story. His insight and commitment to his work have made me proud to be an honorary Takooshian student.

Many others helped me track down pieces of the puzzle the story presented. Michael Farrar, who grew up across the hall from Kitty and Mary Ann's apartment, was my guide to family memories that tell a side of the story no one else knew. His mother, Sophia, was a friend to Kitty. Robert Sparrow recalled the killer he and his father defended fifty years ago, and helped me depict Moseley's role in the story. Barry Rhodes, who represented Moseley years later, proved to be a vital source and a great conversation. Murray and Carol Berger shared their home and their still-vivid impressions of how it felt to live in Kew Gardens after the crime.

My new friends Angelo Lanzone and Victor Horan shared their memories of Queens in the 1960s. Joseph De May provided insights and documents that helped immensely at the outset of my research. Myrna Skoller gave me valuable background to the work her husband, Charles, did and the book he wrote about it. Assistant District Attorney Charles Testagrossa, Professor Andrew Karmen, Dr. Frederick Naftolin, Judith and Alan Gansberg, and Billy Corrado went out of their way to aid my efforts. In Brooklyn, the people of Prospect Heights High School, St. Augustine's Parish, and the Lesbian Herstory Archives provided valuable support. The great Harlan Ellison provided inspiration and perspective. I also owe thanks to Murray Weiss, Curtis Sliwa, Bobby Graves, Anthony Annucci, Bill Genovese, and Al Gatullo.

I count myself lucky to work with Tom Mayer, the best editor a guy could have, and to Tom's colleagues at Norton: the irreplaceable Ryan Harrington, project editor Don Rifkin, designer Ellen Cipriano, and their Norton colleagues Devon Zahn, Eleen Cheung, Ingsu Liu, Loriel Olivier, and Steve Colca. Mary Babcock's sharp eye improved the manuscript. And I'm grateful to John Glusman and Bill Rusin for their support.

Thanks to Anthony Mattero and Matthew Carlini of Vigliano Associates for working with me, and to David Vigliano for representing the book.

No book of mine is complete without a tip of the cap to Ken Kubik of Grass Roots, Inc. and my fellow members of the Kubik Circle, Chris Carson and Doug Vogel. Or to the essential Christina Bloom, Luis Fernando Llosa, Allison Burnett, Liz Halsted, David Barnes, Dr. Patricia Cook, Arthur Kretchmer, Steve Randall, and Jim Kreutzer.

On the home front, I couldn't imagine life without Pamela Marin, author of the brilliant *Motherland*, my in-house editor, partner, and muse. Special thanks to Lily Cook and Cal Cook.

A last nod goes to Abraham Rosenthal. Without his efforts to remind the world of what happened to Kitty Genovese, we probably wouldn't remember her name.

A Note on Sources

Like most nonfiction books, *Kitty Genovese* combines primary and secondary sources. I have had the benefit of thousands of pages of documents, many of them newly discovered after decades of neglect, as well as 140 pages of police records acquired through New York's Freedom of Information Law. I've used the past tense when employing trial transcripts, books, newspapers, and other secondary sources (for example, "Gansberg wrote" or "Sparrow said"). If a source is quoted or referred to in the present tense ("says Lanzone" or "Takooshian believes"), he or she spoke to me during the two years of my research on the book.

Select Bibliography

Barry, Dan. *City Lights.* New York: St. Martin's Press, 2007.

Chernetsky, Michael. *Sergeant: My 34 Years behind the Badge.* Frederick, MD: PublishAmerica, 2008.

Ellison, Harlon. *Deathbird Stories.* New York: Harper & Row, 1975.

Fletcher, Tony. *All Hopped Up and Ready To Go.* New York: W. W. Norton, 2009.

Frommer, Myra Katz, and Harvey Frommer. *It Happened in Manhattan.* New York: Berkley Books, 2001.

Halberstam, David. *The Powers That Be.* New York: Alfred A. Knopf, 1979.

Hurewitz, Daniel. *Stepping Out.* New York: Henry Holt, 1997.

James, Bill. *Popular Crime.* New York: Simon & Schuster, 2011.

Kaiser, Charles. *The Gay Metropolis: 1940–1996.* New York: Houghton Mifflin, 1997.

Karmen, Andrew. *Crime Victims: An Introduction to Victimology.* Pacific Grove, CA: Brooks/Cole, 1990.

Lewis, Barry. *Kew Gardens: Urban Village in the Big City*. Kew Gardens, NY: Kew Gardens Council for Recreation and the Arts, 1999.

Prince, Carl E. *Brooklyn's Dodgers: The Bums, the Borough, and the Best of Baseball*. New York: Oxford University Press, 1996.

Rosenthal, A. M. *Thirty-Eight Witnesses: The Kitty Genovese Case*. New York: McGraw-Hill, 1964.

Ross, Norman, ed. *Official World's Fair Souvenir Book*. New York: Time-Life Books, 1964.

Rotolo, Suze. *A Freewheelin' Time*. New York: Broadway Books, 2008.

Samuel, Lawrence. *The End of the Innocence: The 1964–1965 New York World's Fair*. Syracuse, NY: Syracuse University Press, 2007.

Seedman, Albert A., and Peter Hellman. *Chief!* New York: Arthur Fields Books, 1974.

Skoller, Charles. *Twisted Confessions*. Austin, TX: Bridgeway Books, 2008.

Talese, Gay. *The Kingdom and the Power*. New York: New American Library, 1966.

Van Ronk, Dave, with Elijah Wald. *The Mayor of MacDougal Street*. New York: Da Capo Press, 2005.

Index